GLOBAL BEST PRACTICE

Passing your ITIL® Managing Across the Lifecycle Exam

London: TSO

Published by TSO (The Stationery Office) and available from:

Online
www.tsoshop.co.uk

Mail, Telephone, Fax & E-mail
TSO
PO Box 29, Norwich, NR3 1GN
Telephone orders/General enquiries: 0870 600 5522
Fax orders: 0870 600 5533
E-mail: customer.services@tso.co.uk
Textphone: 0870 240 3701

TSO@Blackwell and other Accredited Agents

First edition 2014
First published 2014

ISBN 9780113314386

Printed in the United Kingdom for The Stationery Office
Material is FSC certified. Sourced from responsible sources.
P002623218 c5 05/14

Contents

List of figures

List of tables

Foreword

Congratulations, you have reached the last stage on your journey to becoming an ITIL Expert. The final step is to take your Managing Across the Lifecycle (MALC) exam. This qualification covers complex topics around managing services across the service lifecycle, and managing the practice of service management across the lifecycle. The exam is designed to test your knowledge of these topics and to enable you to prove this knowledge to yourself and others.

Being well prepared is vital. Designed to supplement your accredited training, you can use this study aid to help prepare for the course and your exam. It introduces the MALC qualification and presents the content in a logical order, based on the learning units in the syllabus. It includes a sample case study and practice questions to help you apply your knowledge.

The next step, of course, is to pass the examination. But hopefully it won't seem too daunting once you have undertaken your accredited training and studied this publication.

What you do after passing the exam is down to you, but you will have demonstrated to the world that you are an ITIL Expert. With this in your toolkit, you will have the skills to help manage services and the service management practice in your own organization, making a real difference to your career and to the business. And your learning doesn't stop there – you will continue to learn as you overcome IT service management challenges in the workplace.

The world of IT service management is open before you and I wish you well.

Peter Hepworth
CEO AXELOS

Acknowledgements

AUTHOR AND MENTOR

Anthony T. Orr, BMC Software   Author
Maggie Kneller, independent consultant   Mentor

REVIEWERS

AXELOS and The Stationery Office (TSO) would like to thank *it*SMF for its help in the quality assurance of this publication. Thanks are also due to those people who generously donated their time in reviewing this title, including:

Claire Agutter, IT Training Zone Ltd; Dag Blokkum, ROI IT LLC; Aslak Ege, Capra Consulting; Ryan Fraser, ServiceNow; Rosemary Gurney, Global Knowledge UK; Shirley Lacy, ConnectSphere; Tricia Lewin, independent consultant; Vernon Lloyd, Somerset Computer Consultancy Ltd; Stuart Rance, independent consultant.

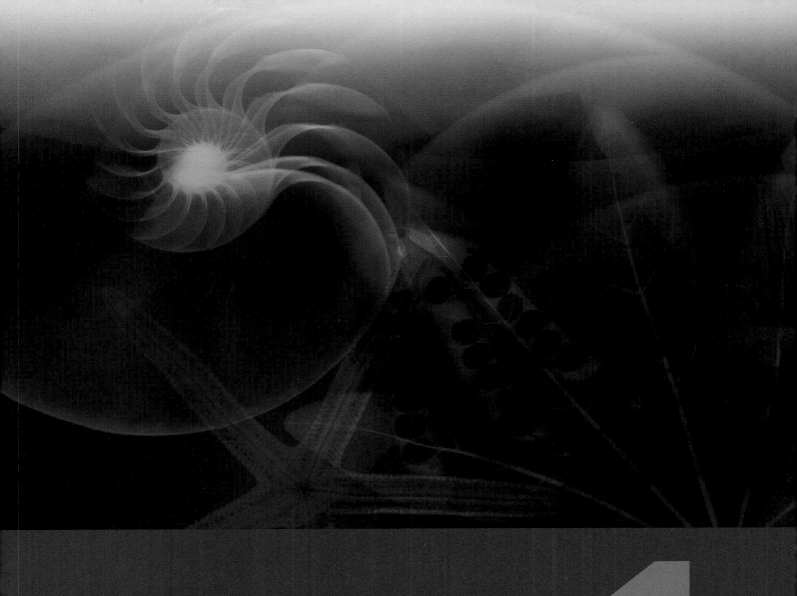

Introduction 1

1 Introduction

The ITIL best-practice framework provides guidance on how people, processes and technology can enhance the quality of IT services. ITIL is applicable to all types and sizes of IT service provider; thousands of organizations are using ITIL best practice. ITIL is a framework for IT service management which organizations can adopt and adapt to suit their own specific needs.

1.1 THE ITIL QUALIFICATION SCHEME

The internationally recognized ITIL qualification scheme comprises five levels of qualification: Foundation, Intermediate, Managing Across the Lifecycle (MALC), Expert and Master. The Intermediate level takes two different perspectives of IT service management – through a service lifecycle stream and a service capability stream. The two streams each have a number of different qualifications and associated learning modules – nine in total. Candidates are likely to take a mixture of modules across both streams. The qualifications and learning modules for the Intermediate ITIL certifications can be seen in Table 1.1.

1.2 THE MALC QUALIFICATION

MALC has a cross-lifecycle, strategic and managerial focus from the two perspectives of:

- Managing services across the service lifecycle
- Managing the practice of service management across the service lifecycle.

Before a candidate can be trained and examined for the MALC qualification, the candidate must have obtained 17 credits or more from the following:

- Two credits from the ITIL Foundation certificate
- Fifteen credits or more from ITIL Intermediate qualifications: each lifecycle module is worth three credits, and each capability module is worth four credits
- Complementary qualification credits and credits from earlier ITIL qualifications where these can be used towards the required amount of credits.

Table 1.1 The two ITIL Intermediate streams

ITIL Intermediate service lifecycle stream	ITIL Intermediate service capability stream
Service strategy (SS)	Operational support and analysis (OSA)
Service design (SD)	Service offerings and agreements (SOA)
Service transition (ST)	Release, control and validation (RCV)
Service operation (SO)	Planning, protection and optimization (PPO)
Continual service improvement (CSI)	

Because the Intermediate qualification is made up of nine different modules, MALC candidates will have acquired their 15 credits from a variety of routes. The modules studied at Intermediate level will have an impact on the most appropriate areas of focus for pre-study in preparation for the MALC course (see section 1.6 for more information on pre-course requirements).

Candidates who attend a formal approved MALC training course with at least 30 contact hours and pass the MALC exam will be awarded a MALC certificate and five credits. This is the final exam candidates need to pass to qualify them to apply for the ITIL Expert certificate.

1.2.1 Intent and target group

The MALC qualification focuses candidates on implementing and using the best-practice framework across the full lifecycle, and on how to manage and deliver services using ITIL. After taking an accredited course, candidates should be able to understand how to apply the service lifecycle to IT service management challenges, improvements, programmes and projects on the job.

The MALC qualification focuses on the application of strategizing, planning, using and measuring ITIL practices in an integrated functioning model, including:

- How the lifecycle stages form an integrated whole
- Process integration and interfaces
- Shared data/information/knowledge.

The MALC qualification is intended for anyone who wants to apply for the ITIL Expert certification and for those involved in the design, development, management, coordination, support, improvement and integration of IT services – particularly consultants and those who are new to, or would like to progress to, a management role. This includes, but is not limited to, chief information officers (CIOs), chief technology officers (CTOs), IT managers, service managers, supervisory staff, team leaders, designers, architects, developers, planners, IT consultants, IT audit managers, IT security managers and IT trainers.

The MALC course and qualification will be of interest to:

- Individuals who require a business- and management-level understanding of the ITIL service lifecycle and how it may be applied to enhance the quality of IT service delivery and support within an organization
- Individuals seeking to attain the ITIL Expert qualification, for which the MALC exam is a prerequisite
- Individuals seeking the ITIL Master in IT service management, for which the ITIL Expert certification is a prerequisite
- Individuals obtaining industry-recognized masters degrees in IT service management from accredited universities.

1.3 FINDING YOUR WAY AROUND THE SYLLABUS

The syllabus is organized into learning units. Each unit identifies the recommended minimum teaching time or approximate teaching time (called 'minimum study period' in the syllabus) to adequately cover the subject. Each learning unit also has an associated level of difficulty for the exam.

Note that training providers may deliver training for the learning units in a different sequence from that used in the syllabus. There is nothing wrong with this. They are encouraged to combine and compile the course materials to provide a logical flow for presenting and teaching the subject. Training providers nonetheless have to ensure that all areas of the syllabus are covered and that training is delivered in a way that supports the stated learning outcomes, the level of difficulty and the minimum study periods.

1.3.1 Learning units

The MALC syllabus is divided into seven learning units:

- **MALC01** Key concepts of the service lifecycle
- **MALC02** Communication and stakeholder management
- **MALC03** Integrating service management processes across the service lifecycle
- **MALC04** Managing services across the service lifecycle
- **MALC05** Governance and organization
- **MALC06** Measurement
- **MALC07** Implementing and improving service management capability.

1.3.2 Core publication references

Each learning unit relates to sections covered by the five core publications that make up the ITIL lifecycle suite:

- Cabinet Office (2011). *ITIL Service Strategy*. The Stationery Office, London.
- Cabinet Office (2011). *ITIL Service Design*. The Stationery Office, London.
- Cabinet Office (2011). *ITIL Service Transition*. The Stationery Office, London.
- Cabinet Office (2011). *ITIL Service Operation*. The Stationery Office, London.
- Cabinet Office (2011). *ITIL Continual Service Improvement*. The Stationery Office, London.

The syllabus contains abbreviated cross-references to the core guidance – for example, SS 6.8.8 would refer to *ITIL Service Strategy* section 6.8.8. This cross-referencing is to help both training providers and candidates refer to, and familiarize themselves with, the relevant sections in the source materials.

1.4 THE MALC EXAM

1.4.1 Level of difficulty

Your training provider should explain the level of knowledge and skill that you need to achieve for each learning unit. In the exam, candidates must be able to demonstrate proficiency at the required level. The exam tests candidates' ability using a methodology called 'Bloom's taxonomy of learning'.

The ITIL qualification scheme and associated syllabuses have been developed using Bloom's levels, and each level of qualification has one or more corresponding Bloom's levels. The Bloom's levels are:

- **Level 1** Knowing
- **Level 2** Comprehending
- **Level 3** Applying
- **Level 4** Analysing
- **Level 5** Evaluating
- **Level 6** Creating.

Candidates for the MALC exam are advised to develop proficiency for all syllabus learning units up to Bloom's level 5. This means that they are expected to be able to do the following in an ITIL context:

- Apply the relevant ITIL practices as a whole and apply the concepts in new situations, both real and imaginary

- Separate concepts into component parts to understand the structure and distinguish between facts and inferences
- Distinguish between possible solutions and decide which approach to take.

MALC is the final mandatory qualification leading to ITIL Expert certification, and as such is at a level above the Intermediate qualifications. The MALC exam is set at Bloom's levels 4 and 5, which are higher than those of the Intermediate exams, which are at Bloom's levels 3 and 4.

1.4.2 The exam

The MALC exam:

- Is 2 hours in duration (or 2 hours 30 minutes for students taking the exam in a language that is not their own native language)
- Consists of 10 questions
- Has a pass mark of 35 out of 50 (70%)
- Is a mix of easy, moderate and hard questions.

The majority of the questions in the MALC exam are based on a case study. Up to two questions in each exam will not reference the case study. Whether the case study is to be used or not will be noted at the start of each exam question. The case study will be given to students by their course provider.

This publication includes an example case study and practice questions. As with the real exam, some of the questions test knowledge across more than one learning unit. Synergies between the learning units and across the service lifecycle must be understood in order to successfully pass the MALC exam.

1.5 ABOUT THIS PUBLICATION

This publication provides guidance to support students in planning, studying and preparing for the MALC qualification. Beyond the exam, the knowledge acquired from the MALC course can also be applied to the delivery of quality service management practices in an organization.

Please note that this publication is intended to supplement, but not replace, the material in the five core ITIL publications and any materials and teaching provided by your selected training provider.

1.5.1 How to use this publication

This publication contains guidance on how to prepare for your course and the exam, and can be used throughout your period of learning – and beyond. Summary information and key illustrations from the five core publications are provided to assist with your learning, along with a sample case study and practice questions.

This publication comprises nine chapters, plus the appendices. Chapters 1 to 9 do not have to be read in sequence, but the information contained in them needs to be understood.

Chapter 1 sets the scene and introduces the MALC qualification.

Chapters 2–8 help you to understand the syllabus learning units as follows:

- **Chapter 2** Key concepts of the service lifecycle
- **Chapter 3** Communication and stakeholder management
- **Chapter 4** Integrating service management processes across the service lifecycle

- **Chapter 5** Managing services across the service lifecycle
- **Chapter 6** Governance and organization
- **Chapter 7** Measurement
- **Chapter 8** Implementing and improving service management capability.

Chapter 9 explains what to expect from the course and exam, and helps you to prepare and plan your studies.

The appendices provide an example case study, and practice questions and answers to help you practise for the exam:

- **Appendix A** Sample case study
- **Appendix B** Sample test questions
- **Appendix C** Answers to sample test questions.

1.6 GETTING STARTED BEFORE THE COURSE

It is recommended that students begin preparing for the course well in advance – at least four weeks before the course starts. By starting early, you will be in a better position to maximize the value of your learning experience. Many training providers provide pre-course reading lists, materials and sample questions. If they do, please use these to guide your reading and learning.

When starting out it is useful to:

- Have access to the core ITIL publications
- Be clear why you are taking the qualification – your motivation to learn depends on the relevance of the learning to you, your education and your career
- Check to make sure you have the prerequisites for the course and exam

- Plan your studying – identify the resources and time allocation that you need to complete the required minimum recommended personal study time of 28 hours
- Think about how much work you need to do to get to the required level of knowledge and performance to maximize your mark in the exam, e.g. target level of difficulty and pass mark. Plan how you can keep track of your improved knowledge and performance
- Buy and read this study guide.

You are advised to do at least 28 hours of pre-course work. You should:

- Obtain a copy of the course schedule and a copy of the MALC syllabus from your accredited training provider, or download it from www. itil-officialsite.com. Read the learning objectives in the syllabus, and understand what they mean and how they support your personal learning and career goals. Identify how you intend to apply your new knowledge in practice.
- Refresh the knowledge you gained at the Foundation level – reminding yourself of the key concepts covered at this level.
- Refresh the knowledge you gained at the Intermediate level.
- Review the terminology list provided in the MALC syllabus. Use it to identify those terms and concepts that you need to revise or study. The terminology list specifies those areas (at Foundation and Intermediate level) that are prerequisite knowledge and will help to focus your preparatory work in the relevant areas. This is important because, depending on the Intermediate qualifications you have taken, you may not have covered all of the concepts that are prerequisite knowledge during your previous studies.

ITIL can be used alongside other best practices and frameworks. To achieve a more holistic understanding of IT service management, a high-level understanding of other best practices is also needed, including project management and application design.

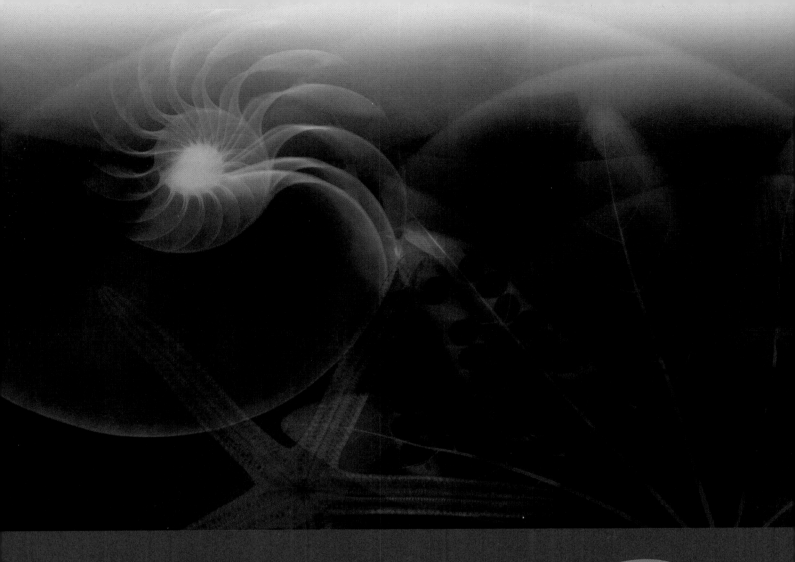

Key concepts of the service lifecycle

2

2 Key concepts of the service lifecycle

This is learning unit ITIL EX: MALC01 of the syllabus. The recommended minimum teaching time for this unit is 3 hours. This unit focuses on the service lifecycle and some key concepts relating to it, and it looks at these concepts from a managerial and strategic viewpoint. This is the basis upon which the other learning units will build. The difference between MALC and the Intermediate qualifications is that now, instead of focusing on one particular lifecycle stage or a specific group of processes, the service lifecycle is considered holistically. This requires an understanding of the relationships between the lifecycle stages. The curriculum in MALC01 should be understood and applied across the other syllabus areas.

You should review the entire service lifecycle and the interfaces and links between the stages, with a focus on managing services from stage to stage. You can do this by applying and understanding service management principles, concepts and the relationships between people, processes, partners and products in the delivery and support of effective and efficient services that provide business value.

Each component of the lifecycle has a unique value to the delivery and support of IT services. Together the various IT components create a value chain to support the desired business outcomes from the service. Organizations that are not receiving the intended business value from their IT services are probably missing a key capability from a lifecycle stage, process or activity. Understanding the architecture of the service lifecycle and how the components work as a system will help you identify

performance improvements which can positively impact business decisions and support and enhance the overall business strategy. Figure 2.1 (from the core ITIL publications) provides an overview of the lifecycle and illustrates how one stage supports the other stages to create a business value chain.

An IT service provider is a specialized organization with specialist expertise. IT's expertise includes the ability to provide factual data about the usage of IT resources in the delivery of IT services to support business outcomes, and then to transform this data into knowledge which can provide valuable information into business decisions and overall strategy.

It is important to remember that IT needs to support and enable business outcomes. IT that is done poorly or inadequately can have a negative effect on the business.

An example to illustrate this is of an organization that is monitoring IT capacity for a particular service. Through the monitoring activity, the capacity manager has identified by analysis (transforming data into knowledge) that, based on current trends, in five months' time the organization will not have enough capacity to support the service. The organization reacts and buys additional capacity to meet the perceived demand. In this case the organization did not consider the future business demand, only the IT trends. The business was not anticipating any new customers for the service. IT has now over-resourced the IT environment, which increases capital and operational cost and indeed the total cost of ownership for providing the service,

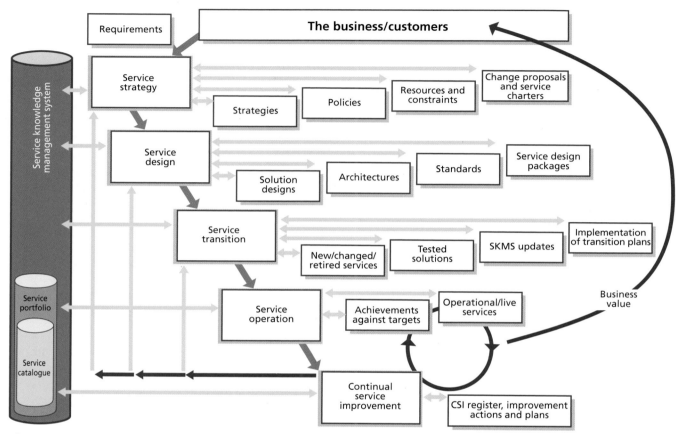

Figure 2.1 Integration across the service lifecycle

thus adversely impacting the return on investment for the service.

IT has to be perceived as a capability of the business and should work in collaboration with the business objectives. An IT department that does not understand the needs of the business will create projects and improvement initiatives based on its own needs instead of supporting business objectives. The vision and mission of the business are likely to be supported by objectives such as 'run more efficiently', 'grow into other markets effectively' or 'create competitive advantage' (see Table 2.1, taken from the core ITIL publications). In the previous example, the costs associated with the additional unneeded capacity should have been avoided. This situation could also be seen as a lost opportunity, since these wasted funds could have been used to grow or add needed services or improvements for the benefit of the business. IT service management, when done well, can contribute to the organization meeting its goals.

Table 2.1 Common business objectives

Operational	Financial	Strategic	Industry
Shorten development time	Improve return on assets	Establish or enhance strategic positioning	Increase market share
Increase productivity	Avoid costs	Introduce competitive products	Improve market position
Increase capacity	Increase discretionary spending as a percentage of budget	Improve professionalism of organization	Increase repeat business
Increase reliability	Decrease non-discretionary spending	Improve customer satisfaction	Take market leadership
Minimize risks	Increase revenues	Provide better quality	Become recognized as a producer of reliable or quality products or services
Improve resource utilization	Increase margins	Provide customized offerings	Become recognized as low-price leader
Improve efficiencies	Keep spending to within budget	Introduce new products or services	Become recognized as compliant with industry standards
Meet contractual obligations	Ensure that performance supports revenue generation	Deliver to meet objectives and obligations	Become recognized as a reliable provider
Reduce customer complaints	Reduce the cost of rework	Improve customer retention	Become recognized as a provider of quality goods and services

The service lifecycle has many components and a defined structure, which is similar to a value chain. Structure can influence or determine the behaviour of the organization, people, processes, services and other components of a service management practice. Organizations operate at different industry maturity levels, with different capabilities and resources. Without an understanding of the service lifecycle structure, how can you manage and deliver a service so that it meets business goals from its inception through to its live operation and finally to its end of life?

Understanding the structure of the service lifecycle helps you manage conflicts in organizational structure that can lead to inefficiencies in the performance of an IT service. A poorly designed organizational structure can sometimes lead to conflicts in roles and responsibilities. There may be multiple functions that have the same level of accountability for an IT infrastructure, with different areas of responsibility. This can result in conflicts when, for example, managing changes to the infrastructure. Releases and deployments will probably affect several teams or functions within the organization, and this can lead to conflicts unless roles and responsibilities are carefully planned. These conflicts can ultimately affect business outcomes.

For example, Tony and Mary work for a financial services organization. Tony works in a function responsible for IT infrastructure, and his manager has given him delegated responsibility to manage changes to the IT infrastructure. Mary works in a different function responsible for data management, including the corporate financial database, and her manager has delegated to her the responsibility for managing changes for that function. Tony believes that if Mary makes a change she should obtain his approval. Mary believes she does not need Tony's approval since she has been delegated authority to make her changes. How would you address this situation? Continue reading as this situation is addressed below.

The service lifecycle can be applied to IT services and their components. It can also be applied to the practice of service management. These two perspectives are important concepts, which need to be understood and are discussed later in this chapter and also in detail in Chapter 4 (Integrating service management processes across the lifecycle) and Chapter 5 (Managing services across the lifecycle).

The definition of a service is: 'A means of delivering value to customers by facilitating outcomes customers want to achieve without the ownership of specific cost and risks.' The official definition adds the following clarification: 'The term "service" is sometimes used as a synonym for core service, IT service or service package.'

In the example, both Tony and Mary deliver an IT service to support a core service. There is no reference to any core service in the example. There could be an implied, but not an explicit, relationship to core services from Tony's and Mary's perspectives. Tony may believe that he is responsible for the core services that are delivered to the customers of the organization. Mary may believe the same, especially since her database may be critical to a core service. Both Tony and Mary are responsible for managing changes in their areas. This could mean that the organization is not service-oriented and not business-focused, since change appears to be managed from an IT component perspective. Tony and Mary are both struggling to do the right things for the business but they are in conflict. The organizational structure, and the roles and responsibilities, appear not to have been designed to take account of the value chain by which enabling services underpin core services that deliver value to the business.

Some organizations, faced with this challenge, create a new function which is sometimes known as a service management office, to help manage changes across multiple business units from a core service perspective. Alternatively it may be more appropriate to change the organizational structure and/or the roles and responsibilities to align with best-practice guidance, introducing ITIL processes, so that this service management practice supports the core IT services for the business. The practice of service management, which includes the organizational structure, roles, skills and competencies as well as processes, helps create organizational collaboration and coordination. In addition, the practice helps organizations become more service-oriented, so that they better understand the relationships between service assets, core services and IT services. This means they can

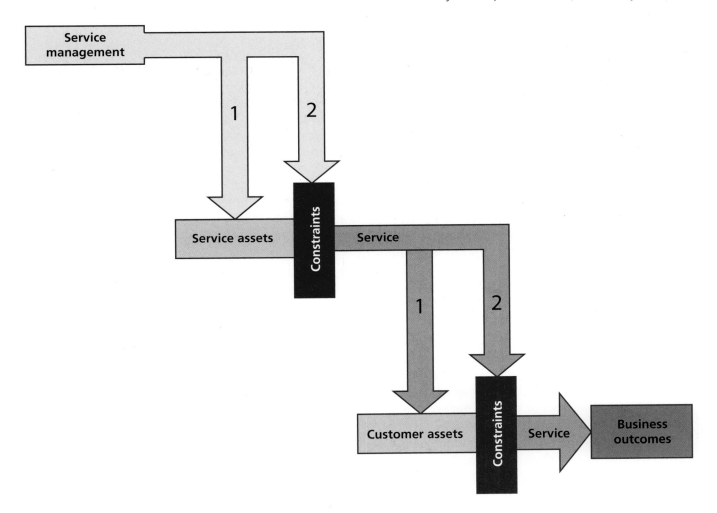

Figure 2.2 Service management optimizes the performance of service assets

manage IT services for business value instead of just managing the IT assets. In the above example there is more focus on managing the IT components by each function than on managing services.

The basic concept of value, including value creation and value realization, will have been covered on Foundation and Intermediate courses, and is

important here. Value creation is achieved through the utility and warranty of IT services. Utility is 'the functionality offered by a product or service to meet a particular need' and can be summarized as 'what the service does'. Warranty is 'assurance that a product or service will meet agreed requirements' and 'refers to the ability of a service to be available when needed, to provide the required capacity, and to provide the required reliability in terms of continuity and security'. Warranty can be summarized as 'how the service is delivered'. When the service has both appropriate utility and warranty, value is created.

Value is not realized until the service becomes operational and is used by the business, creating patterns of business activity or demand. It is assumed that the service has value to both the customer and the service provider, who will always want an increase in value or performance. There are other stakeholders, such as Tony and Mary in the previous example, who contribute to the value of a service. Tony and Mary are a part of the overall value chain for the service. As such, it is important that they work as efficiently and effectively as possible and improve the services they provide to ensure the continued realization of service value.

Figure 2.2 (from *ITIL Service Strategy*) illustrates one of the important concepts of service management. The diagram illustrates that service management increases the performance of service assets used in the delivery and support of services. Service assets are capabilities and resources of the business. These capabilities and resources are expressed within the overall service value chain. Achieving and adding value across the lifecycle stages requires a good understanding of the service value chain. Service management also removes constraints in the delivery and support of services. The services themselves create a relationship between the business and the customer, and between the assets of the service and the assets of the customer. This relationship improves the performance of customer assets and/or removes constraints from the customer, providing utility. The relationship or service offering that is built between the service assets and the customer assets supports business outcomes. This

service offering has to be managed to provide continued value.

Organizations can apply the ITIL guidance as needed within their own unique practice of service management to give rise to a competitive advantage. MALC is about applying the ITIL service lifecycle to IT services and their components and about the overall practice of IT service management. By understanding the current state of their service management practice, and how ITIL can be adopted and adapted to better respond to the challenges and desired capabilities, organizations will be better placed to realize service value.

2.1 MANAGING SERVICES AND SERVICE MANAGEMENT

A service lifecycle approach can be applied both to the practice of service management and to the IT services that are delivered to the customers. MALC considers the service lifecycle from these two perspectives.

2.1.1 The practice of service management

The 'practice of service management' is simply the way IT does its job. The practice of service management is about using the ITIL guidance to develop, operate and improve the organization's IT service management practice. This would include the processes, procedures, organizational structure, functions, roles, responsibilities, skills, capabilities, competencies and resources used in the delivery of IT services. This perspective is considered in more detail in Chapter 4.

Some IT organizations may not be familiar with ITIL as a best-practice framework for IT service management, but this does not mean they do not practise some of its principles and processes. ITIL as a best practice can help improve the IT capabilities for delivering and supporting services.

Service assets are capabilities and resources of the business. Capabilities include management, organization, process, knowledge and people. Resources include financial capital, infrastructure, application, information and people. Service management as a practice is about managing the capabilities, resources and processes relating to each of the service lifecycle stages. It is also about creating a discipline for sustainability within the organization so that assets are optimized towards the delivery of successful business outcomes. Organizations may adopt ITIL and other best practices within their service management practice. ITIL itself is not implemented in the same manner as technology is deployed in an organization. ITIL principles and concepts are applied as a framework for repeating or performing processes and activities in a defined manner. ITIL is non-prescriptive because not all of the advice given needs to be followed to achieve a specific business outcome, and additional non-ITIL guidance or processes can be applied. This non-prescriptive application of ITIL creates a practice unique to each organization, which can result in a unique capability in the management of IT services.

2.1.2 Managing IT services

Adopting and adapting ITIL to manage IT services means taking a service lifecycle approach to the management of services. At the start of the lifecycle, this is executed with the strategy management for IT services process. Services are managed based on a strategy, then the rest of the lifecycle supports the strategy. Service management optimizes the performance of service assets within the portfolio or organization for the services delivered and supported. End-to-end optimization of service performance improves the ability to deliver and support services for the organization, which helps increase the economic value of the service for the markets that it serves. Economic value has to be supported in order to justify and ultimately pay for all the assets consumed by the service.

When managing services, it is also important to understand that the delivery and support of a service revolves around the relationship between the customer and the service provider. Services are defined by the relationship and the exchanges between service provider assets and customer assets, and if there is no relationship, then there is no service. For example, a customer asset can be a person, while a service provider asset can be an application; the person uses the service provider's application, and the service provided is defined in terms of the outcome the application delivers, including warranty. A relationship exists between customer and service provider, defined by the service between the two entities. This service might be a key customer-facing or 'core' service-providing utility, and it might be supported by 'enabling' or supporting services which are also delivered by the service provider but not seen directly by the customer.

> **Example: service management vs managing services**
>
> Joe had a hobby of fixing cars for himself. A friend of his found out about Joe's hobby and asked Joe to fix a car for him. Joe fixed the friend's car and his friend was so pleased that he told all of his friends about how good Joe was at fixing cars. Joe immediately started getting more requests to fix cars – so many that he decided to open a business fixing cars.

He created a business plan, decided which services to offer and the prices of the services. He took his business plan to a financial institution for a loan to start his new business. The financial institution approved his loan. Joe had funding to implement his business design, including all of the IT capabilities that he needed to run his business. The business was set up and began running well. Joe had created his business by having a strategy supported by specialized capabilities so that he could provide value to customers in the form of services. He was able to implement the design of his business, including the introduction and management of quality IT services that met the needs of the business. He then used the outcomes or the framework of his service management and IT service management initiatives to manage the services that were delivered to his customers.

Later, he met a consultant who helped to make Joe's IT capabilities more efficient and effective through the implementation of a service catalogue and better service desk technology for service requests and incident management.

The ITIL service lifecycle principles can be used in whole or in part to help organizations improve their service management practice. Joe, in this case, has delivered and is managing a service. Joe has established a practice for the services that he delivers. Now, he has changed his practice of service management, incorporating improvements. This change has helped him manage the services he delivers more efficiently and effectively.

Joe always delivered services and managed the delivery of services, and once he introduced a process he had a practice of service management. He continues to manage services and to run his service management practice. Part of the practice of service management involves improvement, and he has now started to do this.

2.2 THE SERVICE LIFECYCLE

The service lifecycle is made up of the following lifecycle stages:

- Service strategy
- Service design
- Service transition
- Service operation
- Continual service improvement.

Service strategy provides a basis for every stage of the service lifecycle, and every stage of the service lifecycle should support the service strategy. For example, your strategy will provide principles that will govern the way you manage your service desk, and the service desk should support your overall portfolio, service demand and financial concerns, and operate according to your overall strategy.

For example, an IT organization implements a service desk; the service desk is operational seven days a week, 24 hours a day; the service desk costs $1.5 million a year to operate; the service desk supports three services for the business that serve one unique market; the business's expected total cost of ownership for the service is $1 million a year; the service desk in this case does not support the strategy because of the shortfall of $0.5 million in financial value. The way you decide on the strategy that you have for the business should be realized in the governance of the activities, projects and programmes that are designed, transitioned and made operational by the business. Outcomes from the other stages of the lifecycle can provide guidance for improvement of the overall business strategy. This happens because of the implementation of the strategy and the feedback given to strategy during that particular stage of the lifecycle. This feedback should be a component of a collaborative effort for continual service improvement. The strategy decisions we make for addressing a particular market and the value to all stakeholders should be realized across the lifecycle in the things we do as service providers and the things we do not do related to the service. It is important to quantify value across the lifecycle stages in a collaborative manner to support the overall service value chain.

Although they appear in *ITIL Service Transition*, the change management and change evaluation processes both take place across the entire service lifecycle, with different parts of each process occurring in different stages of the lifecycle. The processes you find in each publication (see Table 2.2) do not all take place entirely within the allocated lifecycle stage. The lifecycle stages and processes do not have such a simple relationship; many of the processes or activities are carried out across two or more stages of the lifecycle, but can be considered to have a 'parent' stage. For example, during the service strategy stage you may actually be executing the change evaluation process when evaluating a

Table 2.2 Processes across the lifecycle

Publication	Processes				
ITIL Service Strategy	Strategy management for IT services	Service portfolio management	Financial management for IT services	Demand management	Business relationship management
ITIL Service Design	Design coordination	Service catalogue management	Service level management	Availability management	Capacity management
	IT service continuity management	Information security management	Supplier management		
ITIL Service Transition	Transition planning and support	Change management	Service asset and configuration management	Release and deployment management	Service validation and testing
	Change evaluation	Knowledge management			
ITIL Service Operation	Event management	Incident management	Request fulfilment	Problem management	Access management
ITIL Continual Service Improvement	Seven-step improvement process				

change to strategy. It is important to recognize and understand the dynamics of the service lifecycle in terms of process interactions and methods of thinking related to decisions and activities in each lifecycle stage. Understanding that a process such as change management or change evaluation is carried out across one or more lifecycle stages helps you to think and act appropriately for the decisions that have to be made within each stage of the service lifecycle. Chapter 2 in each of the core publications (especially section 2.4.2) provides additional information related to this concept.

2.3 SERVICE VALUE ACROSS THE DIFFERENT STAGES OF THE SERVICE LIFECYCLE

Each stage of the service lifecycle creates or contributes value to each IT service and this value is realized during service operation. Service strategy, service design, service transition and continual service improvement are value-creating stages. Within these stages no service consumption occurs, and no patterns of business activity are present. Service operation is where the customer/user consumes the service, resulting in business activity and value realization for both customer and service provider. For example:

- An organization decides to bring a new service to market (service strategy).
- The service is designed to be as efficient as possible, meeting all the customer requirements (service design). Service design is a balance: designing utility and warranty at a cost that the customer and service provider are happy with and willing to agree – rather than meeting all the business requirements. There is always a level of negotiation about what is possible, achievable, acceptable, realistic etc.

- The service is transitioned into production, ready for use, and the organization is ready to operate and support the service (service transition).
- The service is consumed by the customer or user and support is provided; the customer assets are supported by the service provider assets, and value realization occurs (service operation). The business only starts to obtain the required benefit once the service is in live operation.
- Opportunities exist to improve the service based on stakeholder feedback and changing circumstances. Stakeholders include customers, users and the service provider (continual service improvement).

The IT assets that support services (for example, infrastructure components, supporting services etc.) can add value but only if they support services that realize value for the business/customer; otherwise the asset is not needed. Basically, service provider assets that do not contribute to planned or current service offerings to customers should be retired. These assets increase total cost of ownership, reduce return on investment for other services, and affect the organization's overall ability to invest in other services that may be needed to grow or develop the business.

You should ensure that you understand the service value chain, and that the components or assets return value to the business. This will help with understanding cost and determining service price. The value chain consists of core, enabling and enhancing services (see Figure 2.3) supported by capabilities, including the organization and resources, such as the people with specific roles and responsibilities to support the service. This will help the organization understand how each function and role contributes to the service value and supports service decisions.

Service operation is the stage at which value is realized, and where customers use customer-facing services that have gone through the other value creation stages of the service lifecycle. Other stages and processes of the lifecycle affect service operation. For example, the financial management for IT services process has a major effect on the ongoing cost of operations. There are aspects of financial management that are carried out during the service strategy stage, but most financial decisions that will affect the cost of ownership of the service and the operational costs are made in service design. The financial decisions made in the service strategy stage are more related to the overall way an organization funds its IT initiatives relative to the portfolio of services and its approach to business cases and accounting, rather than specific services. Service design may formulate several solutions to meet the needs of the business at different cost points and negotiate the most appropriate cost point and design with the business. This might require returning to the service strategy stage to amend the business case and obtain approval for additional funding if the level of approved funding is not adequate for the suggested service outcome. This is also a good example of a process appearing in one of the core ITIL publications covering a specific stage of the service lifecycle, but also being applied in other stages. Many financial decisions are made during the service design stage, including the whole equation of functionality and warranty versus cost. Also, if design is not done effectively, it will have a huge impact on the cost of operations, affecting return on investment.

Improvements in service operation can affect service strategy and other lifecycle stages. Within service operation, the results from monitoring user satisfaction, IT components and processes can lead to change of current strategy and system design. For example:

- During the service operation stage, user satisfaction surveys are conducted and the IT service provider finds out that users are not happy with the length of time it takes the operations team (application, technical and operation management) to provide a new server.
- Users have also decided to use cloud-based solutions to bypass the need for IT operations to provide new servers.
- Operations immediately implements new technology to provide in-house servers as well as external cloud servers, exceeding the user expectations and helping to reduce IT costs.
- User satisfaction improves dramatically because of the new IT solution.
- The team that is responsible for service strategy changes its service management sourcing strategy, based on the result of the operations team initiative, to a cloud-first strategy for new services within the service portfolio.

2.4 OTHER KEY CONCEPTS

2.4.1 Service component relationships

When managing services, it is important to understand the relationships between service components. The relationships themselves help with modelling services, impact analysis and creating service views for the markets, customers, users or any stakeholder that a service provider serves. Figure 2.3 illustrates the relationship between types of services, such as core, enabling, enhancing and business services. There can be multiple views of the services, depending on who requires the view and the decisions to be made with the information. An example could be a view for a particular customer that might show only those customer-facing services that they directly use. There could also be user views or views of requestable services made available. These views can be displayed as a particular view of a service catalogue or a requestable service catalogue.

These models are used for: understanding cost of service; building a configuration management database with appropriate attributes, scope and detail; designing the architecture of configuration management systems; and the overall construction of a service knowledge management system for decision support. Note in Figure 2.3 that business services can be delivered without IT support. When IT delivers capabilities or resources to support a business service, what IT is actually delivering is in terms of an 'IT service' supported by people, process,

technology, operational level agreements and external contracts. The user or customer of the IT service views the service in terms of utility or its core capability for a specific purpose and does not need knowledge of the IT service supply chain in order to use the service. On the other hand, the customer can have concerns related to the IT supply chain, especially as it relates to regulatory compliance in terms of where data resides.

2.4.2 Service value chain and value network

Services are delivered through a sequence of functions, activities, processes etc. working together, each contributing a specialization to form a chain of events or value chain or value network. The

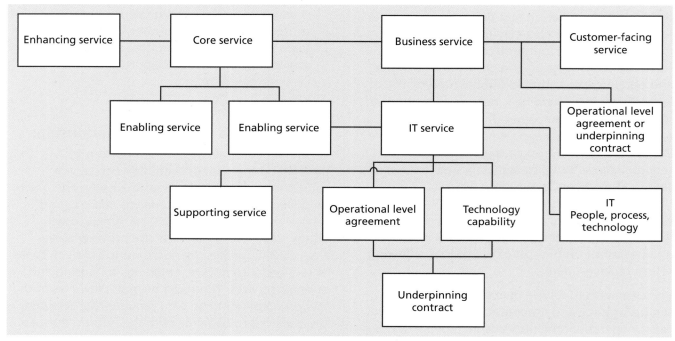

Figure 2.3 An example of service component relationships

definitions of partnership, value chain and value network are given below:

■ A partnership is 'a relationship between two organizations that involves working closely together for common goals or mutual benefit'.
■ A value chain is 'a sequence of processes that creates a product or service that is of value to a customer. Each step of the sequence builds on the previous steps and contributes to the overall product or service.'
■ A value network is 'a complex set of relationships between two or more groups or organizations. Value is generated through exchange of knowledge, information, goods or services.'

The term 'value chain' is used within this publication but you should consider the other terms of value network and partnership when comprehending the content.

2.5 ORGANIZING FOR SERVICE MANAGEMENT

There is no best way to organize people for service management. There are various stages of organizational development that serve organizations in different ways, with different outcomes. The starting point for organizational design depends on the strategy of the organization. The strategy is usually based upon running the business effectively to meet a particular outcome, such as growing the business or taking the business into new markets.

Organizations are usually divided into specialized functions. Functions are teams or groups of people or other resources that are used to carry out one or more processes or activities. Functions can also be used to carry out activities requiring a particular set of skills or a specific area of knowledge. Functions

can perform a single process or activity and be responsible or accountable for such. Functions can also be used in other manners to be consulted or informed about activities. RACI (Responsible, Accountable, Consulted and Informed) models are used to define how functions and the roles within the functions work with each other and within the functions themselves. RACI models help define and clarify activities within a process across multiple functions and multiple roles.

2.6 RISK ASSESSMENT AND RISK MANAGEMENT

Risk is managed differently at different stages of the lifecycle in order to maximize service value. Risks are different at different stages. For a new service, the identification of potential risk begins in service strategy and a plan for mitigation or risk reduction will be formulated. At every other stage, risk is potentially inherent and the plan will be added to and modified accordingly. Policies and procedures for risk management should be identified at each stage.

Risk can be managed using a consistent approach across the lifecycle. To summarize, possible risks are identified and assessed according to likelihood of occurrence and potential damage, as well as possible countermeasures to reduce or remove the risk, and are then managed according to the risk assessment. The basic risk identification model is to identify the asset, threat and vulnerability. The potential countermeasures are identified and plans are put in place to reduce the risk as appropriate. Contingency arrangements are made in case the risk should materialize. An impact analysis is usually done to aid in contingency planning for the risk, because countermeasures and contingency arrangements would need to be cost-justified on the basis of potential business impact. Countermeasures might include options to control the risk, accept the risk, avoid the risk or transfer the risk.

Examples of risks related to the stages of the lifecycle are:

- **Service strategy risks**   Market risk, customers switching providers
- **Service design risks**   Service utility risk, failure to deliver expected benefits
- **Service transition risks**   Service implementation risk, resistance to change
- **Service operation risk**   Service loss risk, inadequate funding.

It should be noted that an IT service in service operation might be prone to a service strategy risk. This could happen if, for example, a customer switches providers, since this puts the operational service at risk.

A service in operation could also be prone to a service design risk. For example, the design might have failed to take into account an important requirement, and the operational service might therefore fail to deliver benefits relating to this requirement.

Because services deliver value only when in service operation, risk management tends to focus mainly on the risks that will materialize when the service is operational. However, the risks need to be considered at each stage of the service lifecycle. Failure to mitigate a risk during service strategy, service design or service transition can lead to risk materialization in service operation, by which time it may be too late to mitigate or reduce the risk.

2.7   KNOWLEDGE MANAGEMENT

Knowledge management is an example of a process that operates across all stages of the service lifecycle. It is the process responsible for sharing perspectives, ideas, experiences and information, and for ensuring that these are available in the right place and at the right time. The knowledge management process enables informed decisions, and improves efficiency by reducing the need to rediscover knowledge. It also enables collaborative service management for stakeholder decision support across the lifecycle. Knowledge management should not be seen as just a service transition process but as a process that works across the lifecycle, enabled by the configuration management database (CMDB), configuration management system (CMS) and service knowledge management system (SKMS), to support all processes.

The ability to deliver and support high-quality services relies on the ability of people to contribute to decisions and make decisions in various situations. These decisions should not be based just on expert opinion but also on shared data and information available to the IT staff. Since the data is shared, a single system instead of multiple silos of information is preferred for effective decision-making. It is often said that if there are multiple sources of the same type of data, then one or more of the sources is likely to be out of date, which could result in a decision maker having misleading information related to a service and making poor decisions.

One of the challenges in managing knowledge is at the data level. Data is transformed into information, and information is transformed into knowledge to support decisions. Data is sometimes kept and collected without understanding its purpose. This can happen because technology is customized to add additional data at one point in time, and as the organization moves from one release of technology to another over time the customized changes move along with the new versions. The organization sometimes forgets why the additional data fields or customizations were needed and becomes afraid to be without them for risk of impacting a service. Organizations should always review data customizations with regard to their relevance to current decision value. Otherwise they can adversely impact service throughput and performance, as well as cost, by the addition of unneeded data elements that have to be stored and maintained in IT systems.

2.8   SUMMARY

MALC01 focuses on key concepts of the service lifecycle. As you look at the curriculum, do not treat the syllabus references as individual silos of information. The references are meant to help you look at the service lifecycle synergies. As you read the ITIL publications based on the syllabus references in MALC01, apply all of the content across the other syllabus units.

Remember the lifecycle is a service lifecycle and not just a set of processes or enabling technologies, so don't think of the materials in MALC01 in isolation. Organizations adopting ITIL sometimes focus on improving a particular process but this does not always achieve improved service value. This means that the focus is on services, although the user of the ITIL materials may only need information on a process, person or technology aspect of ITIL based on the lack of a particular capability to deliver a service. The desired outcome is to enable you to understand the practice of service management and to help you manage services more effectively. The intent is not just management of a particular lifecycle stage, or of a particular process.

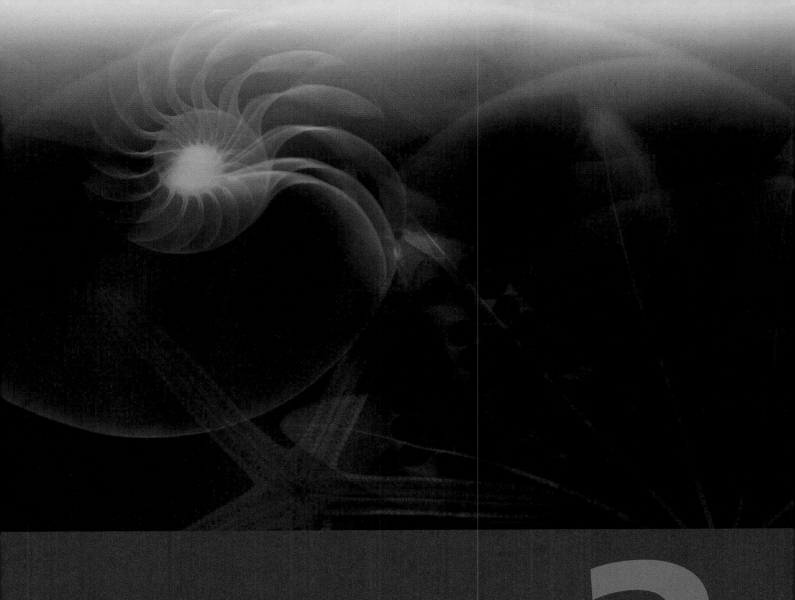

Communication and stakeholder management

3

3 Communication and stakeholder management

This is learning unit ITIL EX: MALC02 of the syllabus. The recommended minimum teaching time is 2 hours. This unit explains the value of good communication and its flow across the lifecycle to ensure the appropriate coordination and collaboration between people involved in delivering and supporting IT services. Communication is one of the things that link the lifecycle stages together. This can include communication between processes which operate in different stages, and also communication between people and teams involved with processes at different stages across the lifecycle. Good communication needs to exist in order for an IT service to move and be managed successfully between one stage and the next.

3.1 COORDINATION OF BUSINESS RELATIONSHIP MANAGEMENT

Good communication helps organizations work as a team. Sharing data and information between functional groups helps with overall service decision support. When done in a collaborative fashion, enabled with technology, communication helps remove independent functional behaviour that may not benefit the service as a whole. Independent behaviour can create constraints and conflict, and can lower overall service performance. Good communication enables dissemination of information and can create harmony between sender and receiver. Effective process interrelationships are based on the output from one process being an effective input into another process. When the output is not effective or needs to be improved, the process owners can resolve the issue through good communication.

There are different types of communication that are important between different parts of the service lifecycle – for example, between the service provider and the business/customers (see Figure 3.1). There are other types of communication that are also important – for example, between different teams or functions within the service provider community. Communication of strategy across the lifecycle is important, as is communication of the result of a particular lifecycle stage to the other stages, as this type of communication aids continuity and continual improvement.

3.2 STAKEHOLDER MANAGEMENT AND COMMUNICATION

If nothing changes, why communicate? In IT there are always changes because of changes in market environment, strategy, customer needs, IT capabilities etc. There are always changing circumstances which are the catalysts for changes. We receive feedback for improvements internally and externally to our organizations. Improvements based on incidents, problems, risk, costs etc. drive our need for change. All these aspects of change require communication both to and from various stakeholders. Changes have to be coordinated properly or the change can adversely affect current

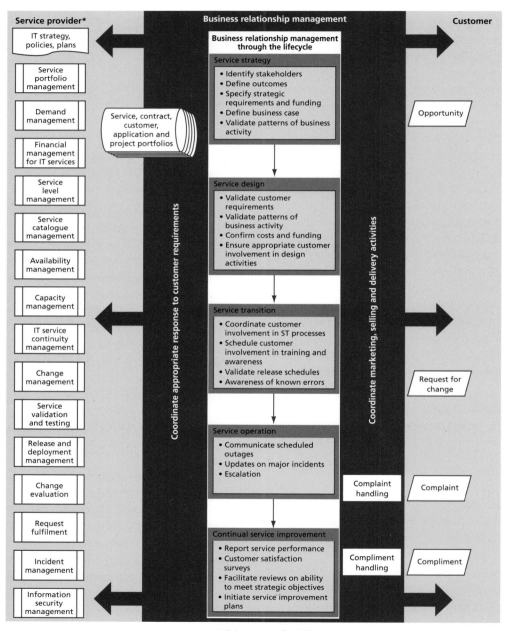

Figure 3.1 Business relationship management activities

operations, resulting in an inability to support business outcomes or value. Good communication is essential to managing change effectively.

Service management stakeholders are people who have an interest in the IT services' outcomes, processes and use of assets (capabilities and resources). They can be anyone involved in delivering or receiving an IT service or affected by the outcome. Stakeholders of an IT service include customers, users, service providers, suppliers of third-party components, and functional teams of people involved in supporting the service. This is not an exhaustive list. It is important to know who the particular stakeholders for an IT service are. This helps with the overall management of communication. It is also important to consider what stake, or interest, each type of stakeholder will have in each IT service. Communication should be appropriate depending on the stake of the particular stakeholder. Simply stated, communication should be for an intended audience with an intended purpose. Outcomes from communication should be to inform, train, provide feedback, coordinate, collaborate and help service decision-making, and you need to consider what role any particular stakeholder plays in order to communicate with them appropriately.

3.3 THE VALUE OF GOOD COMMUNICATION

Each aspect of a communication plan will be appropriate for some but not all stakeholders, since communication should have an intended purpose and an intended audience, and therefore the plan should be tailored to meet the different requirements of different stakeholders. The best approach can come from best practices, past experiences and feedback related to communication improvement. For example, if you know the best way to communicate with a particular stakeholder is through email, then email should be the best practice. Good communication helps create teams and strengthen relationships between teams of people. Figure 3.2 shows the contents of a typical communication plan. It can be used to demonstrate what a good communication strategy across the different stages of the service lifecycle would look like, and how to execute a communication plan.

Figures 3.1 and 3.2 both show the importance of communication between and within all the lifecycle stages, such as: between service strategy and service design; within service design when applying the design coordination process; or within service transition when applying changes. Good communication helps with coordination and collaboration across the lifecycle. Coordinated and collaborative service implementation begins with an organization's strategy and continues through the stages of the lifecycle. A component of a coordinated and collaborative service implementation might be addressing changes through effective communication and stakeholder management. An example of this not occurring might be when a change is approved and the release and deployment team install the change but the service desk is not informed of the change. The change itself could affect service desk technology, which in turn could affect a service that the service desk supports for various stakeholders. The change itself, because of poor communication, could cause service performance to be affected, resulting in organizational reputation issues and other problems.

When communicating with different stakeholders, it is important to understand communication preferences and the importance of listening. How to listen in order to improve communications is an

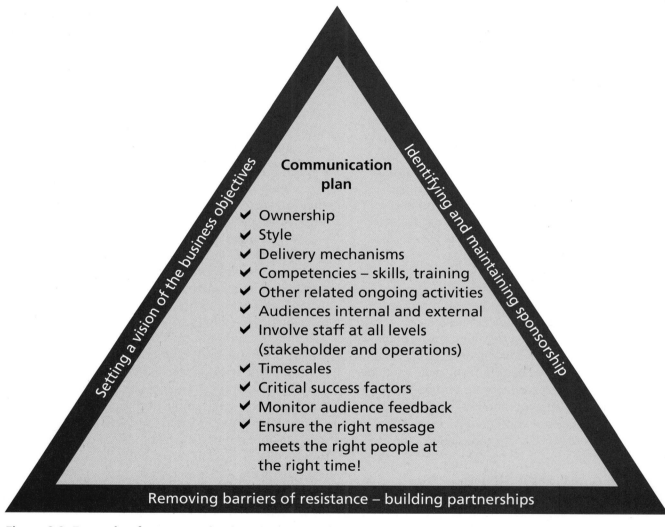

Setting a vision of the business objectives

Identifying and maintaining sponsorship

Communication plan

✔ Ownership
✔ Style
✔ Delivery mechanisms
✔ Competencies – skills, training
✔ Other related ongoing activities
✔ Audiences internal and external
✔ Involve staff at all levels
  (stakeholder and operations)
✔ Timescales
✔ Critical success factors
✔ Monitor audience feedback
✔ Ensure the right message
  meets the right people at
  the right time!

Removing barriers of resistance – building partnerships

Figure 3.2 Example of a communication strategy and plan contents

important aspect of communicating. Communication can be one-directional or bi-directional. Bi-directional communication is considered best practice in most circumstances, so that the sender of the communication can get feedback from the receiver on whether the communication was understood and interpreted correctly. Communication also has to be timely, be targeted at the right audience in the right manner, and communicate benefits for stakeholder buy-in. Who, what, why, when, where and how are typical components of a communication between two parties.

Examples of methods of communication and types of communication across the lifecycle include the following:

■ Service models are useful within, between and across all the lifecycle stages to communicate how people, process, supplier and technology components interact with each other. They can be used to help define services, to conduct impact analysis and performance analysis, and for overall understanding of the service design of changes and improvements.

■ Service design packages (SDPs), architectural documents, plans, strategies and other documents are good communication aids for the passage of information within service design to help with design coordination.

■ In service transition, communication is a challenge when people do not want the transition or do not buy in to the changes. In this case feedback is needed to help design the communication plan to enable buy-in and enable the transition to succeed.

■ In service operation, communication should be part of the day-to-day routine to relay the statuses of operational services, infrastructure components, day-to-day activities, incidents, problems, changes, requests, exceptions, emergencies and other operational statuses.

Methods of communication include speaking, writing, presenting, demonstrating and listening. There are different ways of communicating information, including workshops, training sessions, team meetings, organizational meetings, one-to-one meetings, newsletters, posters, the internet, social media, email and communication devices such as pagers, phones and others.

3.4 SUMMARY

MALC02 focuses on communication and stakeholder management. The key to understanding this section is to consider the many requirements for communication and how the different types of communication to and from various stakeholders are related to the different parts of the lifecycle. Communication needs to be considered between different types of stakeholder, within lifecycle stages, between the different lifecycle stages and across the whole lifecycle.

Special attention should be paid to managing change as it relates to communication and stakeholder value. Good change management depends upon good communication between stakeholders. Poor communication can affect any stage of the lifecycle, which can affect the ability to deliver or support an operational service or the progress towards an operational service. Examples of poor communication are:

■ In service strategy, not completely communicating business outcomes across the lifecycle

■ Within service design, not communicating design coordination activities

■ Between strategy and design, not communicating appropriate design considerations for managing costs

■ In service transition, not communicating changes to operations.

Many more examples exist of bad communication and its effect on service delivery and support. Proper communication is the enabler of organizational coordination and collaboration for effective and efficient services that deliver business value.

Integrating service management processes across the service lifecycle

4

4 Integrating service management processes across the service lifecycle

This is learning unit ITIL EX: MALC03 of the syllabus. The recommended minimum teaching time is 6 hours. This unit's focus is on the practice of IT service management, which means the individual processes and how they operate together. Understanding the theory related to individual processes and how they integrate to support the service value chain is important to ensure that the business gets the expected outcomes from its IT, thus deriving value.

This unit also considers how each process is used so that together they enable a service provider to conceive, build, implement and operate services, then later improve them if required. Managing the practice of IT service management is about how ITIL processes are applied to real IT services.

4.1 THE INTEGRATION OF SERVICE MANAGEMENT

The ITIL processes do not work in a vacuum or siloed manner, but support each other. Each process has defined goals, objectives and activities that deliver service outcomes. Figure 4.1 does not illustrate all the possible interfaces and integrations between processes or stages of the lifecycle but it does illustrate that each process delivers one or more outputs to other processes.

One example of process integration relates to continual service improvement. Continual improvement is based on feedback from each process, using a systematic approach between the lifecycle stages and the processes with the aim of continually achieving the overall goal of efficiency, effectiveness and economic value of services. Other examples, illustrated in Figure 4.1, include: the service desk uses the processes of incident management and request fulfilment; the incident management process generates outputs such as a problem record to the problem management process; and the problem management process generates outputs such as the correction of problems to the change management process. Problem management will also produce output information on known errors to the incident management process. The change management process might create output for an incident request to the incident management process if a change fails.

4.2 THE IMPACT OF SERVICE STRATEGY

Service strategy provides direction for the execution of the other lifecycle stages. This direction defines and governs how the service provider will practise IT service management. Service strategy creates the framework for value creation, which includes the acknowledgement or imposition of constraints in design and governance of transitions. A constraint in service design could simply be the budget allocated to a particular service delivery project. It could be a matter of prioritizing certain quality considerations over cost considerations. Strategy also defines how operations will realize service value

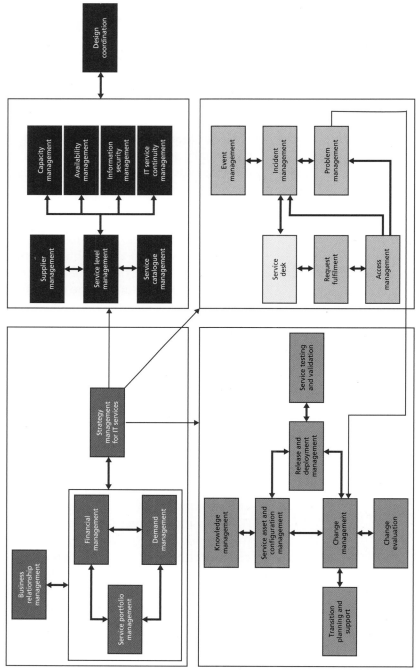

Figure 4.1 Examples of process integrations

for the organization and the customer. Strategy will influence the operational expenditures and capital cost in which operations deliver and support services. Continual service improvement across the lifecycle can be initiated because of strategy changes to help achieve the overall service vision. On the other hand, continual service improvement can influence service strategy by feeding back improvement suggestions from other lifecycle stages that result in strategy changes. The strategy changes can then affect the rest of the service lifecycle.

Service strategy influences the inputs and outputs across each stage of the lifecycle and in specific processes that create the service value chain. This value chain drives service utility and warranty. The creation of a service is based on the service provider's assets working efficiently to produce the service. This involves specialized outputs from one process being appropriate inputs into another process. Services are usually created through projects, and the way that project management controls the scope, time, cost and overall quality of the service is influenced by service strategy. Service strategy also influences the way that effective communication, planning, governance, people, processes, products and partners combine during service development so that the resulting service provides value.

4.3 THE VALUE OF A SERVICE LIFECYCLE WHEN DESIGNING SERVICE SOLUTIONS

Every process matters in the delivery and support of services. Organizations that are facing business service challenges may find that they are missing key activities within a process or missing an entire process that is needed for the services to perform as desired. The value of each process to the business outcomes must be understood in relation to the business challenges and how the processes work with each other. A change to one process or an activity may improve the outcome of a service. Caution should be taken to avoid changing or managing technology or a process that has no effect on the service. Service providers may find themselves making technology changes or process changes without focusing on the service outcome. Sometimes it is difficult for service operations to know whether a change has an impact on the business outcome, when the operational team has no insight into what the business service needs are. So, in this case, service operations may find themselves doing operational process management or operational technology management, not service management. For example, a service provider may change the technology that it uses and still not meet the needs of the business or the IT strategy, or it may improve a process but still have a constraint or missing activity or process that affects the service value.

Designing a service solution requires an understanding of all the components that make up the service (see Figure 4.2, taken from *ITIL Service Design*). When improving the design of a service solution, the current state of the service needs to be understood, as does the desired outcome and where in the service value chain to apply the needed changes for the desired outcome. The 'where' to apply the changes requires understanding of the service lifecycle and the capabilities of the lifecycle components. This understanding helps service providers apply the appropriate solution for the recognized problem.

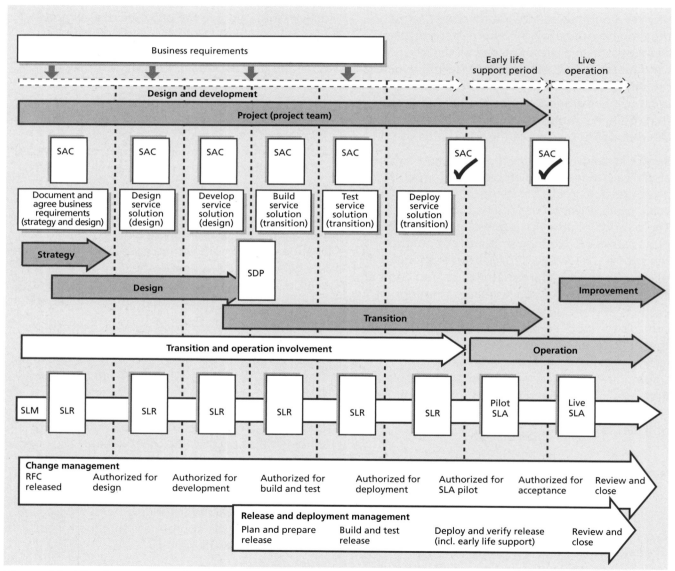

Figure 4.2 Aligning new services to business requirements

4.4 THE INPUTS AND OUTPUTS OF PROCESSES AND STAGES

Review Table 4.1 (taken from the appendices of the core ITIL publications) and note which outputs from one service lifecycle stage become inputs to other lifecycle stages. This table illustrates clearly that there is integration between the processes across the lifecycle. You will see that vision and mission from the service strategy stage is output to all stages; note also that knowledge and information is input from the service knowledge management system (SKMS) to all stages of the lifecycle. This tells you that all stages need to be aware of the vision and mission from service strategy so that the correct direction is set for the processes and activities across the lifecycle. It also illustrates that the SKMS is a central source of information shared by the different processes across the lifecycle to support decisions related to the inputs and outputs of each lifecycle stage.

Table 4.1 Examples of inputs and outputs across the service lifecycle

Lifecycle stage	Examples of inputs from other service lifecycle stages	Examples of outputs to other service lifecycle stages
Service strategy	Information and feedback for business cases and service portfolio	Vision and mission
	Requirements for strategies and plans	Strategies, strategic plans and policies
	Inputs and feedback on strategies and policies	Financial information and budgets
	Financial reports, service reports, dashboards, and outputs of service review meetings	Service portfolio
	Response to change proposals	Change proposals
	Service portfolio updates, including the service catalogue	Service charters including service packages, service models, and details of utility and warranty
	Change schedule	Patterns of business activity and demand forecasts
	Knowledge and information in the service knowledge management system (SKMS)	Updated knowledge and information in the SKMS
		Achievements against metrics, key performance indicators (KPIs) and critical success factors (CSFs)
		Feedback to other lifecycle stages
		Improvement opportunities logged in the CSI register

Table continues

Table 4.1 *continued*

Lifecycle stage	Examples of inputs from other service lifecycle stages	Examples of outputs to other service lifecycle stages
Service design	Vision and mission	Service portfolio updates, including the service catalogue
	Strategies, strategic plans and policies	Service design packages, including:
	Financial information and budgets	■ Details of utility and warranty
	Service portfolio	■ Acceptance criteria
	Service charters, including service packages, service models, and details of utility and warranty	■ Updated service models ■ Designs and interface specifications
	Feedback on all aspects of service design and service design packages	■ Transition plans ■ Operational plans and procedures
	Requests for change (RFCs) for designing changes and improvements	Information security policies
	Input to design requirements from other lifecycle stages	Designs for new or changed services, management information systems and tools, technology architectures, processes, measurement methods and metrics
	Service reports, dashboards, and outputs of service review meetings	Service level agreements (SLAs), operational level agreements (OLAs) and underpinning contracts
	Knowledge and information in the SKMS	RFCs to transition or deploy new or changed services
		Financial reports
		Updated knowledge and information in the SKMS
		Achievements against metrics, KPIs and CSFs
		Feedback to other lifecycle stages
		Improvement opportunities logged in the CSI register

Lifecycle stage	Examples of inputs from other service lifecycle stages	Examples of outputs to other service lifecycle stages
Service transition	Vision and mission	New or changed services, management information systems and tools, technology architectures, processes, measurement methods and metrics
	Strategies, strategic plans and policies	
	Financial information and budgets	Responses to change proposals and RFCs
	Service portfolio	Change schedule
	Change proposals, including utility and warranty requirements and expected timescales	Known errors
		Standard changes for use in request fulfilment
	RFCs for implementing changes and improvements	Knowledge and information in the SKMS (including the configuration management system)
	Service design packages, including:	Financial reports
	■ Details of utility and warranty	Updated knowledge and information in the SKMS
	■ Acceptance criteria	
	■ Service models	Achievements against metrics, KPIs and CSFs
	■ Designs and interface specifications	Feedback to other lifecycle stages
	■ Transition plans	Improvement opportunities logged in the CSI register
	■ Operational plans and procedures	
	Input to change evaluation and change advisory board (CAB) meetings	
	Knowledge and information in the SKMS	

Table continues

Table 4.1 *continued*

Lifecycle stage	Examples of inputs from other service lifecycle stages	Examples of outputs to other service lifecycle stages
Service operation	Vision and mission	Achievement of agreed service levels to deliver value to the business
	Strategies, strategic plans and policies	
	Financial information and budgets	Operational requirements
	Service portfolio	Operational performance data and service records
	Service reports, dashboards, and outputs of service review meetings	RFCs to resolve operational issues
		Financial reports
	Service design packages, including:	Updated knowledge and information in the SKMS
	■ Details of utility and warranty	Achievements against metrics, KPIs and CSFs
	■ Operational plans and procedures	Feedback to other lifecycle stages
	■ Recovery procedures	Improvement opportunities logged in the CSI register
	SLAs, OLAs and underpinning contracts	
	Known errors	
	Standard changes for use in request fulfilment	
	Information security policies	
	Change schedule	
	Patterns of business activity and demand forecasts	
	Knowledge and information in the SKMS	

Lifecycle stage	Examples of inputs from other service lifecycle stages	Examples of outputs to other service lifecycle stages
Continual service improvement (CSI)	Vision and mission	RFCs for implementing improvements across all lifecycle stages
	Strategies, strategic plans and policies	Business cases for significant improvements
	Financial information and budgets	Updated CSI register
	Service portfolio	Service improvement plans
	Achievements against metrics, KPIs and CSFs from each lifecycle stage	Results of customer and user satisfaction surveys
	Operational performance data and service records	Service reports, dashboards, and outputs of service review meetings
	Improvement opportunities logged in the CSI register	Financial reports
	Knowledge and information in the SKMS	Updated knowledge and information in the SKMS
		Achievements against metrics, KPIs and CSFs
		Feedback to other lifecycle stages

4.5 THE VALUE TO THE BUSINESS AND THE INTERFACES OF ALL PROCESSES

The process areas and their value to the business are summarized in Table 4.2. This information can be helpful for identifying process gaps in a real service situation. For example, if the business is having a problem making choices about appropriate IT service investments, there is likely to be a need for the service portfolio management process; if the business has a concern that IT service changes are too costly, there may be a problem with the change management process or problems within service design.

Table 4.2 Business value and interfaces of ITIL processes

Lifecycle stage	Process	Value	Interfaces
Service strategy	Strategy management for IT services	Helps to decide the direction of the service provider and align this to the direction of the business; ensures that the use of resources, capabilities and investments is aligned with business priorities	All service management processes to provide: ■ Direction and governance ■ Guidance for a framework for the service portfolio Financial management for IT services for return on investment (ROI) Service design for policies and constraints Service transition for prioritization and evaluation of services Knowledge management Service operation for execution of strategic priorities Continual service improvement (CSI) for evaluation of strategy execution
	Service portfolio management	Helps the business make sound IT investment decisions	Service catalogue management to determine services in catalogue Strategy management for IT services for overall strategy of services Financial management for IT services for ROI calculations Demand management for information about patterns of business activity Business relationship management to obtain business information and requirements for defining services and ROI Service level management for assuring services achieve the required levels of performance Capacity management for requirements Availability management for requirements IT service continuity management (ITSCM) to identify business impact of risks Security management to ensure confidentiality, integrity and availability objectives Supplier management for risk

Lifecycle stage	Process	Value	Interfaces
	Service portfolio management *continued*	Helps the business make sound IT investment decisions	Change management for evaluation of resources
			Service asset and configuration management for tools, information and data
			Service validation and testing to ensure service functionality
			Knowledge management for decision support
			CSI for feedback on service usage for improvement
	Financial management for IT services	Helps with management of organizational resources to fulfil objectives and ensures IT investments are cost-justified	All processes for cost and benefit
			Strategy management for IT services for financial objectives
			Service portfolio management for service structure for cost models
			Business relationship management for understanding business measurements for value
			Capacity management for technology and service performance options
			Availability management for technology and service performance options
			Change management for determining financial impact
			Service asset and configuration management for information about assets and configuration items (CIs) for analysis and reporting
			CSI for determining if improvement is worth investment
	Demand management	Achieves balance between the cost and business value of a service	Strategy management for IT services to identify key business outcomes
			Service portfolio management to create and evaluate service models, forecast utilization, identify users of service
			Financial management of IT services to forecast cost
			Business relationship management to obtain business activities of customer
			Service level management to formalize agreements with customers

Table continues

Table 4.2 *continued*

Lifecycle stage	Process	Value	Interfaces
Service strategy *continued*	Demand management *continued*	Achieves balance between the cost and business value of a service	Capacity management to match supply with demand
			Availability management to determine when service availability is most important
			ITSCM to perform business impact analysis
			Change management for impact of changes
			Service asset and configuration management to identify relationships between demand on services and demand on systems and devices
			Service validation and testing to ensure patterns of business activities are appropriate to capabilities
			Event management for information about patterns of business activities
	Business relationship management	Gives the service provider the ability to articulate and meet the business needs of customers and to drive business satisfaction with IT	Strategy management for IT services to identify market spaces
			Service portfolio management to identify detailed requirements about the customer environment
			Financial management for IT services to obtain information about the financial objectives of the customer
			Demand management to validate patterns of business activity
			Service level management to understand customer priorities
			Service catalogue management to identify the basis for discussions, reviews and requests from the customer
			Capacity management and availability management for information about outcomes and requirements
			ITSCM for priorities and outcomes
			Change management for impact and priority of changes
			Release and deployment management, and service validation and testing to assure customer involvement
			CSI to validate and prioritize improvements

Lifecycle stage	Process	Value	Interfaces
Service design	Design coordination	Enables the production of consistent quality designs and service design packages (SDPs) for desired business outcomes	Service portfolio management to provide a service charter
			Change management to produce a change request
			Financial management for IT services for details of the value proposition
			Business relationship management to provide desired outcomes
			Transition planning and support to provide an SDP
			Strategy management for IT services to provide service strategy
			Release and deployment management to manage planning and execution of changes
			Service validation and testing to plan and execute tests
			Change evaluation to determine performance of change
			Service level management to define and agree service level requirements
			Availability management, ITSCM and information security management to provide design activities
			Supplier management to ensure suppliers are managed
	Service catalogue management	Provides a central source of information on IT services delivered to customers	Service portfolio management to determine which service will be chartered
			Business relationship management to define the service and customer relationship
			Service asset and configuration management to ensure the configuration management system (CMS) and service catalogue are linked together
			Service level management to negotiate service warranty
			Demand management to determine service packages

Table continues

Table 4.2 *continued*

Lifecycle stage	Process	Value	Interfaces
Service design *continued*	Service level management	Provides a consistent interface between the business and the service provider to define service level targets to meet business requirements. Ensures targets are met and underpinned by supporting services, and service attributes are agreed at a price/cost which is affordable and acceptable to both parties, thus delivering the value/cost balance	Business relationship management to ensure the service provider has a full understanding of the needs and priorities of the business
			Service catalogue management to provide information about services and interfaces
			Incident management to provide data to demonstrate performance against service level agreements (SLAs)
			Supplier management to help define, negotiate, document and agree terms of underpinning services with suppliers
			Availability management, capacity management, ITSCM and information security management to help define service level targets
			Financial management for IT services to validate predicted cost
			Design coordination to ensure design activities are completed
			Seven-step improvement process for identified improvements
	Availability management	Ensures that the availability of systems and services match the needs of the business	Service level management to validate availability targets
			Incident and problem management for resolution of availability incidents and problems
			Capacity management to support resilience and availability
			Change management to help create the projected service outage (PSO)
			ITSCM to assess business impact and risk
			Information security management to define security measures and policies for design
			Access management to provide a method for granting and revoking access

Lifecycle stage	Process	Value	Interfaces
	Capacity management	Ensures that the capacity of systems and services match the needs of the business	Availability management and capacity management to determine resource needs
			Service level management to help determine capacity targets
			ITSCM to assess business impact and risk
			Incident and problem management for resolution of capacity incidents and problems
			Demand management to identify means to influence demand
	IT service continuity management	Ensures that the continuity of the system and services match the needs of the business (business continuity management)	Change management for impact of changes on plans
			Incident management and problem management for agreement on invocation of ITSCM plans
			Availability management for assessment and implementation of risk coordination
			Service level management to agree on recovery requirements in SLAs
			Capacity management to ensure that there are sufficient resources for recovery
			Service asset and configuration management to document infrastructure and relationships in the CMS
			Security management to assess security breaches

Table continues

Table 4.2 *continued*

Lifecycle stage	Process	Value	Interfaces
Service design *continued*	Information security management	Ensures that an information security policy exists, is maintained and enforced, and fulfils the needs of the business	Service level management to assist in determining security requirements
			Access management to grant or revoke access according to security policy
			Change management to assist with assessment of changes
			Incident management and problem management for resolution of security incidents and problems
			ITSCM for assessment of business impact and risk
			Service asset and configuration management to provide accurate asset information
			Availability management for security considerations
			Capacity management for security considerations
			Financial management for IT services for funding approval
			Supplier management for managing access to systems and supplier responsibilities
	Supplier management	Provides value for money from suppliers and contracts and ensures that all targets in contracts and agreements are aligned with business needs by underpinning the SLAs	Service level management to provide targets, requirements and responsibilities
			Change management to manage changes to supplier agreements and documents
			Information security management to set policy for supplier access to services and systems
			Financial management for IT services to provide funding approval
			Service portfolio management to document supplier relationships in the portfolio
			ITSCM to manage continuity of suppliers

Lifecycle stage	Process	Value	Interfaces
Service transition	Transition planning and support	Ensures the ability to handle high volumes of changes and releases	Demand management to provide resource requirements
			Service portfolio management to provide input to planning
			Business relationship management to help manage communication with customers
			Supplier management to ensure appropriate contracts are in place
			Service asset and configuration management, release and deployment management, service validation and testing, change evaluation and knowledge management to ensure they are coordinated by this process
	Change management	Mitigates risks from changes; implements changes that meet customer needs at the right cost	Transition planning and support to coordinate transitions
			Release and deployment management to release and deploy changes
			Change evaluation to evaluate significant changes
	Service asset and configuration management	Optimizes performance of service assets and configurations	Change management to identify impact of proposed changes
			Financial management for IT services to capture cost and other data
			ITSCM for awareness of assets
			Incident management and problem management to maintain data relating to incidents and problems
			Availability management to use configuration data for impact analysis
	Release and deployment management	Delivers change faster at optimum cost; ensures customers/users can use services that support business goals	Design coordination for creation of SDP as input
			Transition planning and support to provide framework for releases
			Change management to authorize work for release
			Service asset and configuration management to provide CMS data and updates
			Service validation and testing to ensure testing is done

Table continues

Table 4.2 *continued*

Lifecycle stage	Process	Value	Interfaces
Service transition *continued*	Service validation and testing	Ensures that the new/changed service can deliver the value/outcomes that it was designed to provide	Release and deployment management to support and to ensure testing takes place
			Change evaluation for change decisions
			Service design coordination to ensure designs are testable
			CSI for improvement ideas
			Service operations for maintenance testing
			Service strategy for funding and resources
	Change evaluation	Establishes the benefit of significant changes through a formal process of assessment of risk and issues and learning from outcomes	Transition planning and support to ensure resources are available
			Change management to determine evaluation needs
			Design coordination to obtain information about the service
			Service level management to understand the impact of issues
			Service validation and testing for required input for evaluation
	Knowledge management	Ensures management and sharing of data, information and knowledge to support decisions related to the delivery and support of services; reduces the need to rediscover knowledge	All service management processes to build a service knowledge management system (SKMS)

Lifecycle stage	Process	Value	Interfaces
Service operation	Event management	Provides early detection of incidents, reducing the need for service outages for resolution	Any process that requires automated monitoring and control
			Incident management for inputting detected incidents
			Problem management for detected problems and faults
	Incident management	Achieves lower downtime for the business; manages business priorities; identifies improvements	Service level management to understand agreed level of service
			Capacity management to provide performance information and performance-related incident resolutions
			Availability management to provide availability of information of services
			Information security management to provide security for information and resolution of security-related incidents
			Service asset and configuration management to provide data for incident management
			Change management for requests for change (RFCs)
			Problem management to investigate and resolve underlying causes of incidents and provide information on known errors
			Access management when unauthorized access attempts are made
	Request fulfilment	Provides quick and effective access to standard services; centralized service fulfilment	Financial management for IT services for cost management
			Service catalogue management for request synchronization with the catalogue
			Release and deployment management to predefine releases
			Service asset and configuration management for updating the CMS with changes
			Change management to log RFC
			Incident and problem management to relate to requests
			Access management for access requests

Table continues

Table 4.2 *continued*

Lifecycle stage	Process	Value	Interfaces
Service operation *continued*	Problem management	Provides a higher availability of services; better business productivity from using IT; reduces incidents	Financial management for IT services for cost of resolving problem
			Availability management to reduce downtime
			Capacity management to address performance issues
			ITSCM to assess impact and provide contingency measures if a major problem escalates to a disaster
			Service level management for improvement of service levels
			Change management to ensure that RFC is done
			Service asset and configuration management to identify faulty CIs in the CMS
			Release and deployment management to deploy problem fixes
			Knowledge management to update the known error database (KEDB) in the SKMS
			Seven-step improvement process to provide basis for improvement
	Access management	Provides controlled access to services; compliance with security policy	Demand management to identify resource needs
			Strategy management for IT services to determine centralized versus decentralized strategy for access
			Security management to provide policies for access management
			Service catalogue management to provide methods and means for access
			ITSCM in case of business disruption
			Service level management for agreement relating to service access
			Change management to control requests for access
			Service asset and configuration management to identify data storage of CIs
			Request fulfilment to provide methods and means for requesting access

Lifecycle stage	Process	Value	Interfaces
Continual service improvement	Seven-step improvement process	Ensures current and future business outcomes continue to be met by identifying and implementing appropriate and timely improvements aligned with changing business needs	All service lifecycle stages

4.6   SUMMARY

MALC03 focuses on the service management processes. The processes provide value for the business, but this value must be understood as it relates to the overall service value chain. There are defined inputs and outputs between the different processes and within them, and between and across the lifecycle stages. Service management as a practice is about having a cohesive set of processes that work together across the service lifecycle. This does not mean that a change to a single process cannot positively affect an IT service and business outcomes. However, the service provider needs to consider the effect of each change on the whole service value chain and its value in terms of an improved overall service performance and business outcomes.

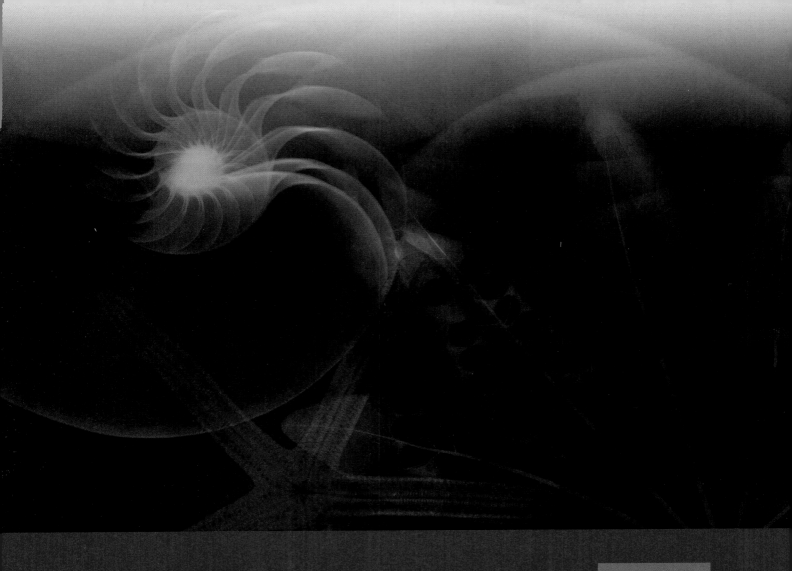

Managing services across the service lifecycle

5

5 Managing services across the service lifecycle

This is learning unit ITIL EX: MALC04 of the syllabus. The recommended minimum teaching time is 6 hours.

Whereas the previous unit was about the practice of IT service management and the processes, this unit focuses on the IT services (and their components – see Table 2.2). An IT service is the focus of the IT service management practice and the ITIL guidance. IT services are what provide value for the business. Without IT services there would be no point in having an IT service management practice.

5.1 VALUE CREATION

An important focus of this unit is how to prioritize and manage IT services from the perspective of business value. Value is created during the service strategy, service design, service transition and continual service improvement stages. Value is realized during the service operation stage. All IT services and components of IT services must have business value and not just IT value. For example, an IT manager buys several servers just because there is budget to do so; the manager adds the servers to the network; the servers support no services; there is a cost for the servers but they add no value to the business. It is important that service components are managed with a clear understanding of business priorities. Focusing merely on IT value without considering the overall stakeholder value can cause harm to the business goals. IT services and

components need to be managed appropriately to ensure that the strategy is realized and that overall customer and business needs are met.

5.2 THE SERVICE LIFECYCLE AS APPLIED TO AN IT SERVICE

This unit is about managing IT services across the service lifecycle. In other words, it is about taking an IT service from concept, through design and development, through transition, and into operation, where it is likely to remain for most of its life and be improved from time to time, and then eventually put into retirement.

While the unit focuses on IT services as they go through the service lifecycle, the concepts discussed here also apply to individual components of an IT service, such as the components of IT infrastructure. Components undergo their own lifecycles – from the decision to purchase or create the component to its eventual replacement or retirement.

An IT service goes through five lifecycle stages (see Figure 5.1):

- **Service strategy** Initially a decision to create an IT service and to provide the service to a specific set of users will be part of a strategy.
- **Service design** The service is then designed and developed with the intention that it will be fit for purpose and fit for use, and that it will meet business objectives, once it is operational.

- **Service transition** The service undergoes a controlled transition to service operation, in such a way that the live operational environment is prepared so that the design will be realized in operation.
- **Service operation** The IT service is used and delivers the required benefits to the business.

- **Continual service improvement** During its operational life, the IT service is likely to undergo improvement as circumstances change.

Eventually the IT service will be retired from operation.

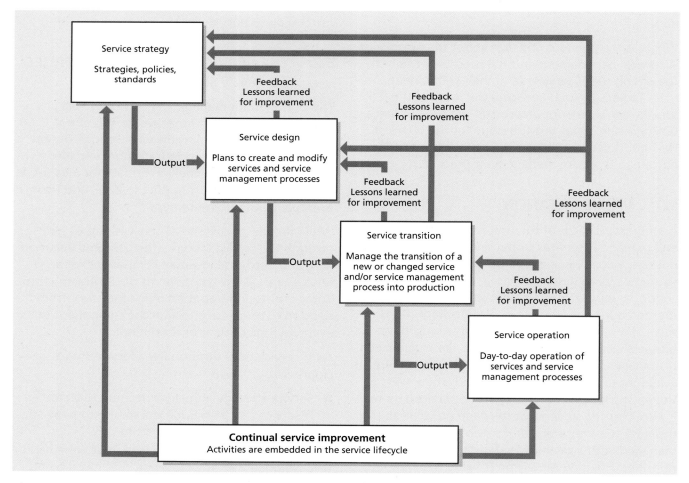

Figure 5.1 Continual service improvement and the service lifecycle

5.3 RISKS FOR AN IT SERVICE THROUGH THE LIFECYCLE

A typical IT service will spend most of its life in service operation. If it has been created with an appropriate strategy, and if it has been well designed, developed and transitioned according to good practices, then it should operate in the way it was intended and provide the expected benefits for the business and therefore deliver business value. However, if there are issues during the early stages of the lifecycle, such that good practices are not followed, then this can lead to difficulties when the service is operational. For example, it can lead to poor availability of service and uncontrolled costs, and the service can fail to deliver the benefits that the business was expecting.

The ITIL service lifecycle requires that IT services are considered from a strategic perspective in terms of business alignment, that they are properly designed and developed according to the design, and that the operational environment is prepared and the service transitioned according to design. This is important in ensuring that the IT service is reliable once operational, that it is available for use, and that its cost is acceptable and under control. It ensures that the business, the customer and the user are satisfied (by getting what they expect and what was agreed), and that the relationship between IT and the business is good (with regard to this particular service).

Once an IT service is operational there may be many reasons why circumstances change – for example, there may be opportunities for improvement. The continual service improvement stage of the lifecycle reflects the fact that operational IT services should be improved when circumstances change if the improvement is justified.

To manage an IT service through the five stages of the lifecycle involves different focuses at each stage and a particular focus at the interface between each stage. It is especially important to manage and control the risks that occur at the interface from one stage to another. One reason that the interfaces can incur risks is because it is common for different teams to have responsibility for different stages.

For example, there might be a strategy team, a development team and an operations team with different reporting lines within an organization, and this can lead to loss of knowledge or information between teams, and differences in understanding of the service, particularly if there is no clear handover between one team and the next. ITIL processes provide mechanisms to reduce the risks at the interfaces between stages – for example, the service design package (SDP) provides a link between service design and transition, and early life support helps to ensure that the skills from service design and transition are available in the early days of service operation. Processes such as change management also provide a link between the different lifecycle stages to reduce risks.

5.4 IDENTIFICATION AND ASSESSMENT OF CUSTOMER AND STAKEHOLDER NEEDS

It is important to identify and assess customer and stakeholder needs and requirements in relation to the IT services at appropriate stages of the service lifecycle and to ensure that they are given appropriate priority. Although high-level requirements are gathered during the service strategy stage, most requirements are gathered in the service design stage. Requirements for minor changes and requests would be gathered during service operation. Reviews take place through the service lifecycle, and particularly when the service is operational – for example, within the service level management process. When in operation, services are subject to continual service improvement, which utilizes the CSI register to record and prioritize potential improvements.

Each stakeholder may have a different perspective on each service. It is important to understand the relationship between the perspectives. For example, a business stakeholder may not understand the limitations of IT, but with the IT stakeholder expressing their needs related to the service, there may need to be a compromise for service delivery. Other examples include a datacentre approaching its limit in the use of power for its IT devices; or a business stakeholder wanting services which would require additional capacity at this particular datacentre. Only when each party understands each other's needs and constraints, and the relationship with other priorities, may compromise be achieved.

5.5 THE SERVICE DESIGN PACKAGE

The SDP has a key role in providing a link between service design, service transition and service operation for any IT service. Its purpose is to ensure that the key elements of design for an IT service find their way through transition and into operation, so that the operational IT service meets its intended design and delivers the expected business benefits and value. The SDP is one of the tools that ITIL gives us to help reduce the risks associated with an IT service going from one lifecycle stage to another. Even if the IT service is handed over from the responsibility of one team to another, the SDP helps to ensure that the important aspects of design are transferred, and therefore that the appropriate knowledge is protected and maintained. For example, if during service transition all the design

requirements are not documented in the SDP, there will be errors in transition that will affect service operation value.

Coordination and collaboration across the lifecycle is important and the SDP provides the link between the stages for each IT service. Service design assigns the responsibility of the SDP to the design coordination process owner. This helps the various roles in the lifecycle understand expectations and activities related to project planning, inputs, outputs, accountability, responsibility and how the IT service needs to function once in operation. Service providers that do not have a communication mechanism such as this may find themselves challenged to manage across organizational functions from a service perspective. These service providers may typically find themselves structuring their organization based on organizational function – for example, based around technology or technical skills. This could potentially create silos of initiatives and activities that are not service-focused. Service-oriented organizations operate in organizational teams in a matrix fashion to support a service or group of services, rather than just supporting a function without insight into the key business drivers for the service.

The SDP contains information such as business requirements from service strategy, functional requirements from service design and the service design itself, a readiness assessment for service transition, a service lifecycle plan, a transition plan, an operational plan and acceptance plans with service acceptance criteria. An important part of the SDP is the service lifecycle plan. This plan explains how the service will move through the stages of design to transition, and from transition to operation, and it includes timescales and phasing for service transition, service operation and for any subsequent improvement of the service. The SDP also lists stakeholders, roles and responsibilities, communication plans, training plans and policies. The SDP, as a formal tool, helps with the efficient and effective coordinated implementation of new services, changes to existing services and service retirements using organizational service assets. Some service providers have implemented services without a formal SDP by using expert knowledge and various formal documents within different stages of service development. A formal SDP helps to reduce the risks associated with the movement of services between lifecycle stages by connecting the activities of the entire service lifecycle into a single formal document which acts as a blueprint for service development and transition into operation (see *ITIL Service Design* Appendix A for complete details of the contents of the SDP).

5.6 MANAGING CROSS-LIFECYCLE PROCESSES

It is important to have the right knowledge, skills and experience when an IT service passes from one lifecycle stage to another. For example, when one team hands over to another, what information is required to be transferred? One of the tools that helps is the SDP (discussed above), and another is early life support, which particularly helps when the developers might otherwise disappear before any operational issues are discovered.

Operational and business staff should be involved early during the design and development of a service, before the service becomes operational. One important aspect of involvement is in a training and testing capacity. If staff are not trained before a service becomes operational because the organization assumes that the service changes will not cause any impact or require any training, then this can lead to operational incidents and problems, and service disruption. The organization will be better positioned for service success if training occurs before the service is in live operation. Organizations that do not include business users or support staff in testing may find that the service does not function as desired when in production, and issues with utility and warranty may go undiscovered until it is too late. Users of the service sometimes use the service in a different manner than the developer or even the customer perceived. Involving business users and support can give an 'outside-in' perspective to help with overall service quality.

As discussed earlier, the service lifecycle is dynamic and feedback is provided between each of the stages. The flow of data, information and knowledge between stages is important for supporting the decisions that need to be made by each role and function that supports the IT service. Stakeholders across the lifecycle are either consuming information or providing data to support a service. This data needs to be normalized, translated and centralized for efficiency and ease of access; hence the service knowledge management system (SKMS) is used across the lifecycle for decision support. The ability to make collaborative decisions throughout the service lifecycle is important for managing service outcomes. Learning and collecting data from actual services moving across the lifecycle can actually help you to improve your IT service management practice and processes, with beneficial impact for all services. It is important to involve stakeholders in managing each service to get the most appropriate feedback to inform improvements and to understand the current service status. Service rehearsals also help stakeholders to visualize the service and provide a better understanding of the roles, actions and activities of stakeholders, their communication needs and expected outcomes. Rehearsals can also help test the overall service model to identify potential improvements. During the rehearsal, shortcomings in the model or the potential for improved efficiency by elimination of an activity may be discovered.

You will need to consider the inputs and outputs between each of the lifecycle stages. Managing across the lifecycle requires that people, processes, partners and technology work in a collaborative fashion, supporting each other and providing feedback to each other. Effective and efficient organizations use their processes to work across company functions with a common interest in the IT services to support business outcomes.

Managing an operational IT service often gives rise to the opportunity for improvements. It is important to consider the service value of any improvement from the customer and user perspective. Customers will not pay for a service that they cannot use and users will not use a service (although a customer may pay for it) that does not help them perform their jobs effectively and efficiently.

5.7 IMPLEMENTING AND IMPROVING IT SERVICES

New IT services and changes to IT services are implemented by going through the various stages of the service lifecycle, from service strategy through service design and service transition into service operation, as discussed earlier in this chapter. Service transition is critical to a successful implementation. As a lifecycle stage, service transition is where the new or changed IT service moves from being under development into operational service. As a collection of processes (the processes listed in *ITIL Service Transition*), it defines those which

execute the whole implementation, from strategy to operation. Each process in service transition plays a critical role in the success of the service in operation. For example, change management helps manage risk, while release and deployment management ensures the training of stakeholders so that they are prepared when the service is operational. Early life support is particularly important for successful implementation, especially for critical services. Without a transition strategy and plan, the IT organization may find itself doing unnecessary work, risking company funds and reputation, not supporting business outcomes, and a number of other issues related to failed IT service implementations.

In terms of improving services, it is important to gain insight into what improvements are needed and justified. The following information (internal to the organization) can provide useful input: customer and user satisfaction surveys; IT metrics such as trend analysis; feedback from service reviews etc. External information such as market trends, technology changes, and changes to regulations is also useful to identify potential improvements to services.

When considering service improvements, service providers need to understand their constraints and the constraints of the organization. This is illustrated in Figure 5.2, which shows that constraints create a set of boundaries that can limit desired outcomes. Some improvements may not be possible because of the organizational limitations and constraints. The diagram shows how capability and resource constraints relate to the overall assets that are used for realizing the service strategy. Service strategy is executed through the service lifecycle and has to be managed within the internal and external constraints to the business. Requirements have to be considered relative to the constraints, risks and desired outcomes across the lifecycle in order for the service value chain to be effective.

5.8 THE CHALLENGES, CRITICAL SUCCESS FACTORS AND RISKS

IT organizations are very complex; they have complex organizational structures, complex processes and complex use of technology. All of these components, including those provided by external suppliers, interact with each other and need to be coordinated. Complexity creates silos of specialization and organizational behaviour, with each person in the organization usually trying to do the best they can to support the business objectives. When service complexity is not coordinated and efficient, the service is usually delivered at an increased cost. Service economics can become very hard to control and manage.

Organizations use business impact analysis and risk assessments to help identify potential issues and risks and make IT services more effective. Many different types of risk are faced by organizations, such as: market risk related to their overall strategy; design risk related to service utility and warranty; and operational risk related to service transition and value realization.

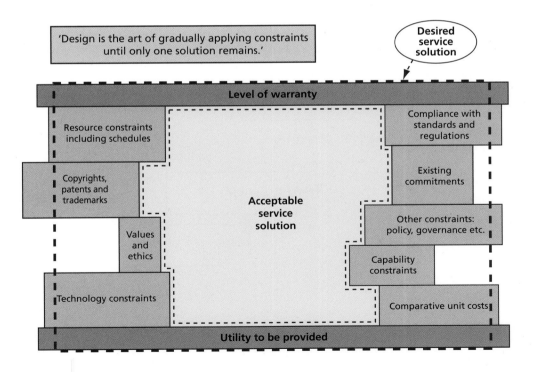

Figure 5.2 Design constraints driven by strategy

Critical success factors (CSFs) are defined in the ITIL glossary as 'something that must happen if an IT service, process, plan, project or other activity is to succeed'. Key performance indicators (KPIs) are the most important metrics that would be 'used to measure the achievement of critical success factors'. For example, the effective management of risks might be a CSF for the business. CSFs can also be based on IT capabilities and resources such as people skills, funding and the use of technology.

For each IT service it would be appropriate to identify the CSFs and have some KPIs which are measured regularly and used to quantify at a high level the success or otherwise of the IT service. Each ITIL process has CSFs and KPIs that can be used to determine whether the process is working effectively, and it is important to consider the CSFs and KPIs in relation to each IT service as it undergoes various ITIL processes. Monitoring CSFs and KPIs can provide useful information about potential and required improvements to IT services.

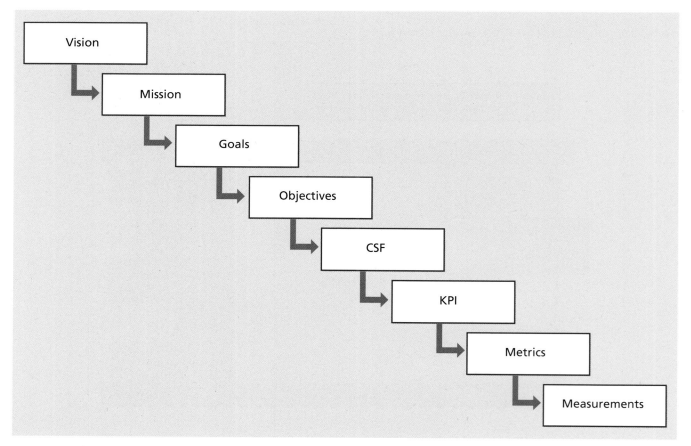

Figure 5.3 From vision to measurement

Figure 5.3 shows the relationship of CSFs and KPIs to other service elements. Monitoring CSFs and KPIs can provide useful information about potential and required improvements to IT services. The elements mentioned in the diagram are related to each other and to the seven-step improvement process, and have an overall connection with business outcomes. Organizational challenges and risks are related to each element.

Some examples of CSFs and KPIs for individual processes are listed below (see the core ITIL publications for lists of others):

- Strategy management for IT services
  - CSF – Identify constraints on ability of service provider to meet business outcomes
  - KPI – Number of corrective actions to remove constraints
- Design coordination
  - CSF – An accurate and consistent SDP
  - KPI – Reduction in number of revisions of the SDP
- Change management
  - CSF – Optimize business risk
  - KPI – Reduction in number of failed changes
- Event management
  - CSF – Ensure events are communicated to the appropriate function
  - KPI – Number of events that require human intervention.

5.9 SUMMARY

MALC04 focuses on managing IT services through the service lifecycle. Each IT service delivers outcomes to customers, which means that to be effective we have to know what the customer wants and is willing to pay for. Otherwise, we may miss the opportunity to provide the appropriate service or we might provide a service that does not satisfy the customer. When planning and designing an IT service, there are key challenges and risks to take into consideration and competing alternatives that may not all achieve the required business value, so priorities have to be set and service investment choices made accordingly. We also have to manage the delivery and support of each IT service through the service lifecycle in order to achieve operational value. There are key processes and activities for accomplishing this, such as design coordination, service lifecycle planning within the SDP, service level management, customer/user satisfaction surveys, and review of trends to determine service improvement decisions.

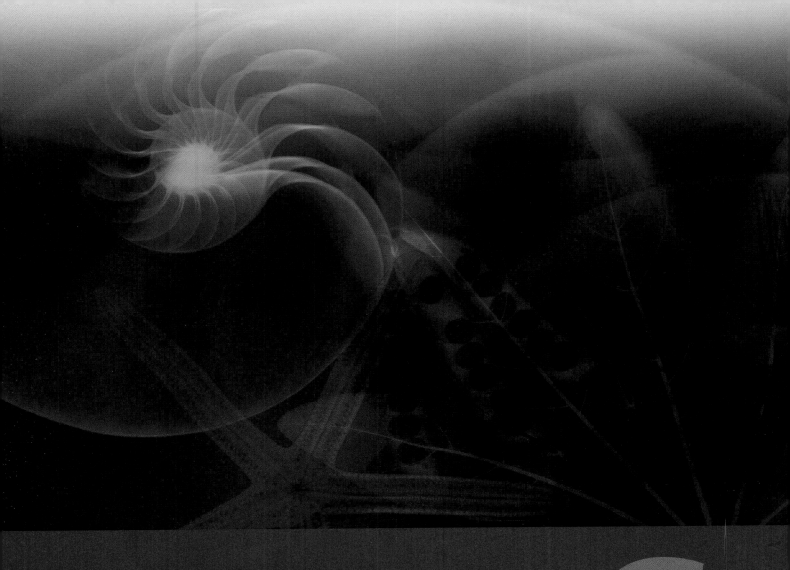

Governance and organization

6

6 Governance and organization

This is learning unit ITIL EX: MALC05 of the syllabus. The recommended minimum teaching time is 3.5 hours. This unit is about governance and organizational structure for the management and delivery of IT services.

6.1 GOVERNANCE

Governance, by definition in the ITIL glossary, 'ensures that policies and strategy are actually implemented, and that required processes are correctly followed'. The glossary also states that 'governance includes defining roles and responsibilities, measuring and reporting, and taking actions to resolve any issues identified'. Organizations behave based on how they are governed, and organizational structure is an expression of governance. Organizational structure expresses specialized roles and responsibilities dictated by the organization's leadership or governors. Governance is mostly a proactive activity and compliance is a reactive response to governance.

Organizational structure is a representation of a value chain of interrelated functions, roles and processes. The processes that create the relationships between the functions and roles established by the

Figure 6.1 Strategy, policy and plan

organizational structure have policies associated with them. The policies help govern the activities of the knowledge workers involved in the particular process. Some policies will focus on the requirement for compliance to process. Each knowledge worker in an organization follows one or more formal or informal processes which have formal or informal rules that govern their activities and also their use of organizational resources such as technology.

Policies are organizational requirements that must be followed. Measuring and reporting helps to show whether or not policy rules are complied with. Governance creates the overall framework within which IT organizational assets are used to deliver the business outcomes. For the IT service provider, governance provides a structure for how IT services are designed, delivered and supported in order to meet business objectives.

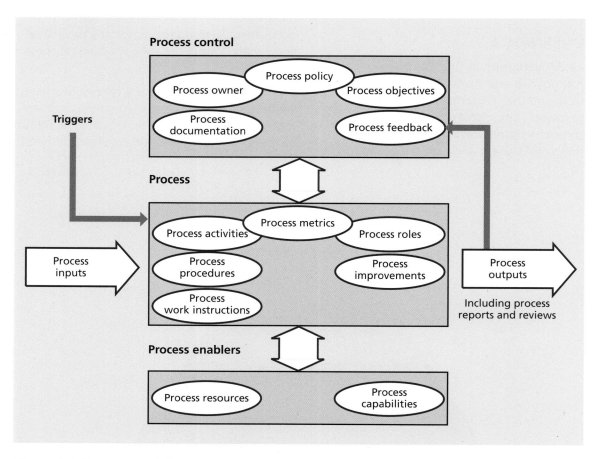

Figure 6.2 Process model

Organizational strategy relating to IT services is defined within *ITIL Service Strategy* as part of the strategy management for IT services process, and is executed using service management across the lifecycle. Execution of strategy across the lifecycle is performed by people, processes, partners and technology. Process is the key component of the value chain that creates the relationships and ties people, partners and the use of technology together to execute the strategic plan in delivering IT services. Processes also create relationships between the lifecycle stages. Figure 6.1 (from *ITIL Service Strategy*) and Figure 6.2 (from Chapter 2 of the core ITIL publications) can help you relate organizational strategy to the execution of processes across the service lifecycle. The basic components of a process are input/trigger, activities and output. Output from one process is input to another for the delivery of the service to a customer. This exchange from output to input creates a value chain tying function, roles and people together through executing processes in order to deliver a service.

It is important to have good governance of both service management and services. Governance helps to define how the organization works to meet its objectives and how services help to meet the organization's objectives. Organizations need to understand their current situation before attempting to improve governance. Consider, for example, an organization making changes in its reporting structure without understanding the effect on the services that are delivered; because the organization does not understand its service value chain, this change may adversely affect its ability to deliver a highly desired service. Governance affects organizational behaviour and sometimes the organization may not know what aspects of governance are affecting behaviour. Audits and change evaluations can help with this assessment

of behaviour. The change management process and the service transition stage can be used, and indeed so can the rest of the service lifecycle where appropriate, to change or transform organizational behaviour.

6.2 ORGANIZATIONAL STRUCTURE, SKILLS AND COMPETENCE

An organization may find that it is missing capabilities or resources which it needs in order to fulfil its strategy. To rectify this it may choose to:

- Build the capability internally through mentoring, training and development
- Acquire the resource internally through hiring resources
- Buy both the capability and resource internally through hiring skilled resources
- Use a third-party supplier to fill the gap by hiring external contracted resources or buying a service from a third party
- Or any combination of these.

Whatever the choice from the list above, the decision should be governed by policy, and the roles and responsibilities need to be clear in order to have value in the current organizational structure for the delivery and support of services.

There needs to be clear accountability and responsibility within the organization for the accomplishment of objectives without conflict between roles and functions, and this is particularly important for the governance of projects. One way of accomplishing this is through the creation and use of a steering group.

Several roles are defined in ITIL. Some are generic and some are specific to a lifecycle stage or process. The generic roles are:

- **Generic service owner** Provides a single point of accountability for a service.
- **Generic process owner/manager** Responsible for the operation of a process – each ITIL process can have a process owner. For example, there could be a service catalogue process owner.
- **Generic process practitioner** Responsible for carrying out one or more activities of a process. This role is sometimes referred to as a knowledge worker in this publication.

There are many organizational structures that can work effectively to achieve organizational goals. The first step to improve the organizational structure is to understand the current organizational state. It is then necessary to determine the desired state, and then to execute the required change to achieve the desired state.

Organizational structures can develop and change over time, particularly as the organization grows and becomes more mature, or needs to face different situations. The stages of organizational development in terms of maturity are defined as network, directive, delegating, coordinated and collaborative. Each stage can serve an organization well depending on the situation and desired outcomes. Each stage of development can have various organizational structures:

- A **network** organization's focus is on speed and it has very few formally defined processes. People in this type of organization move quickly, following their own processes, and there is usually a lot of duplication of work effort. This might be the case in a new, relatively small organization, where processes have yet to take shape and people can communicate with each other easily.
- A **directive** organization's focus is functional success, with basic processes in place. This style of organization often occurs when network organizations get bigger and more complex and look to establish a more formal structure. It can also be typical of a family-run business or an owner-run organization. People in this type of organization do not tend to take initiatives for improvement.
- A **delegating** organization tries to innovate but struggles between functional and process improvement. People in this type of organization are not coordinated with business and IT objectives. This type of organization can develop from a directive organization when it gets even bigger – the 'owner' cannot control everything directly and needs to delegate. It can create silos of activity which are uncoordinated and can lack economies of scale.
- A **coordinated** organization uses formal systems to create greater coordination between the different functional areas and groups of people. People in this type of organization can lack agility.
- A **collaborative** organization is where different groups and functions work in collaboration, and processes work across different functions and teams. So, for example, IT would work in collaboration with the business, and IT could be considered as a capability of the business. People in this type of organization work very effectively in teams.

6.3   SERVICE PROVIDER TYPES AND SERVICE STRATEGIES

Service provider types are defined by ITIL as Type I – internal service provider, Type II – shared service provider, and Type III – external service provider. Type I is internal to the specific business unit for which it provides services. This type may duplicate some of the services provided by other Type I service providers in other business units. Type II service providers are internal to an organization and provide services to multiple business units within that same organization. This type is sometimes the result of multiple Type I service providers being consolidated, although sometimes Type I providers can be created by devolving parts of a Type II provider to be closer to specific business units. Type III service providers are external, meaning that the customers and businesses they serve are external to their organizations. These service providers tend to belong to organizations whose core business includes IT service delivery. Type III service providers offer outsourced services to other organizations and are sometimes created when an internal IT service provider is devolved into a separate service company. Type III service providers can provide services to one or more customer organizations.

It should be noted that IT service providers will also use Type III providers (suppliers) to provide components of services and some of the supporting and enabling services that underpin the IT services they deliver to customers.

The nature and style of governance will depend on the type of service provider. For example, if an aspect of an IT service is outsourced to a Type III provider, it will then be necessary to govern the inputs and outputs from/to the supplier and ensure that the outcomes underpin the requirements for service delivery. The ITIL supplier management process is relevant here.

When looking for resources to fill gaps in capabilities or shortages, it is important to remember that the choice of service provider type must be appropriate for the current and proposed service value chain. The choice of service provider type needs to be based on the organizational strategy, which includes considerations such as environmental conditions, demand and financial aspects, and overall service economics.

Choosing between service provider types usually involves the following types of decisions:

- **Functional reorganization** The business has decided that the current organization structure (Type I) is not meeting its needs. This could be because of duplication in roles, the need for better accountability, regulatory compliance etc. Organizations sometimes perform this type of reorganization to create a service management office – Type II gaining economies of scale and standardized processes to support multiple business units.
- **Corporate reorganization** Shared services are reorganized to provide better support to Type I service providers. This could be to cut costs, improve the quality of services or centralize aspects of service such as support.
- **Value net reconfiguration** The business usually decides this in order to be leaner and cut the costs of duplication or remove inefficiencies in the current value net. Type II or III service providers are usually chosen for this type of change.
- **Aggregation** Shared-service Type II service providers are created to improve process or cost. This could be another example of a reason for the creation of a service management office.

■ **Disaggregation** There is a need for Type I exclusive support; for example, instead of a central service desk supporting multiple offices, each office will have its own service desk. This can provide more localized support, which might be appropriate for specialized parts of the business or to respond faster to business-critical demands.

■ **Outsourcing** A Type III service provider is used to cut costs or take advantage of a specialized service that the business does not want to build or maintain itself.

■ **Insourcing** This involves the removal of an outsourced Type III provider and a change to Type I or II, usually because of cost effectiveness or because a service has become very strategic or requires a level of confidentiality or responsiveness which would be too risky or costly to outsource. Sometimes this also happens because an organization is dissatisfied with an outsourced provider, or in preparation for retendering for a new Type III provider.

6.4 SUMMARY

MALC05 focuses on governance, roles, people, competence and the organization. Governance helps influence the way that services are delivered and determines the organizational structure and the roles and responsibilities. Service providers may choose different provider types to provide specific services or components of services, based on the way that they can most effectively govern the organization's value chain and deliver services to achieve business outcomes. People and roles differ from organization to organization, depending on how the organization is governed. Capabilities and resources can also differ from organization to organization depending on governance.

Organizational governance can be a competitive differentiator in the delivery and support of services. Governance affects process policy, which affects the behaviour of people and the effectiveness of processes within an organization. Service providers must choose how to govern for the best service results based on constraints, environmental factors and other considerations.

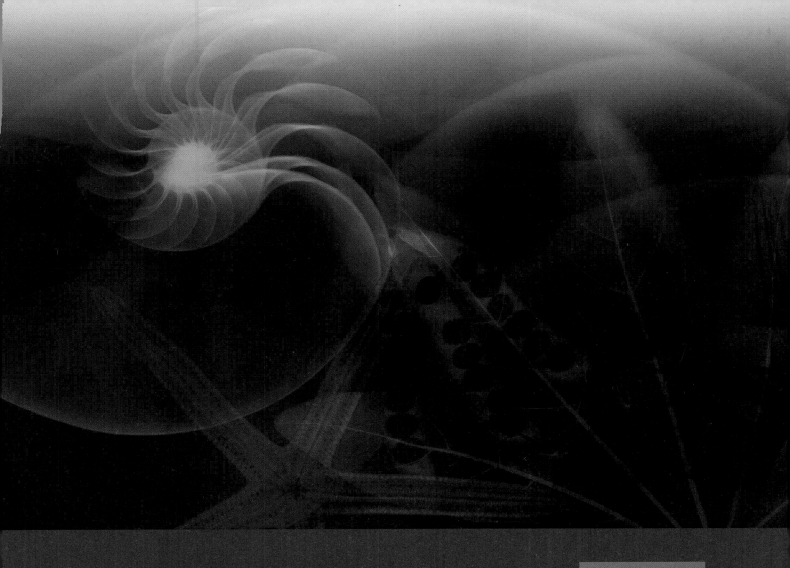

Measurement 7

7 Measurement

This is learning unit ITIL EX: MALC06 of the syllabus. The recommended minimum teaching time is 2.5 hours. This unit's focus is on the measurements to assess a service, to ensure that what was agreed is indeed being delivered to the customer and to inform potential improvement. Measurements also help with continual improvement of the practice of IT service management.

Once a service becomes operational it needs to be monitored and measured to make sure it is delivering its promises. The measures we obtain for a service affect our response to the service. If the service is behaving appropriately, no response is necessary unless the user of the service expected something different. In that case expectations need to be set or the service may need improvement. If the service is measured and found not to be behaving as expected, appropriate responses are usually documented in the service level agreements. In this case, there could be a design flaw that is impacting our ability to deliver the service as promised, so we need to improve the design.

Measurement helps us understand challenges with service delivery. It can also help us proactively understand our customers' needs. By measuring the number of user requests for a particular service or service capability, we can identify demand and, if necessary, consult with our customers to inform them of the need and understand whether anything needs to be changed. By measuring and obtaining service data trends, we can be proactive with our changes for service improvements.

Most service provider organizations cannot survive when viable competition or alternatives come into existence without improving the delivery of services to their customers. Measurements help us to understand whether improvements in service delivery and support might be needed. ITIL can help an organization to get things right first time and be better than the competition and viable alternatives. Most externally facing organizations focus a great deal of effort on improvement in relation to the competition. Improvement may not make the organization the market leader but it does keep it in the market. For internal service providers, improvement helps to keep them in that position when external options or Type III providers exist.

For external service providers, providing a good-quality set of services to external customers helps them to retain these customers and find new ones. Therefore, unless they operate in a monopoly with no risks, continual improvement is crucial. For internal service providers, providing a good-quality set of services to the business is important for the success of the business to which the service provider belongs. The objectives for an internal service provider will align with the business objectives of its customers, and this means that improvement should always be a consideration when it is cost-justified.

Improvement in one stage of the lifecycle or in a particular process or an activity within a process can affect the entire set of services if the improvement relates to a service performance constraint. Measurements across the value chain help identify constraints in the service. If a service component is improved but in an area where there was not a constraint, the service will not necessarily perform any better. Indeed, such 'improvements' can have the effect of not improving the service but making it worse. For example, if a performance improvement increases the ability to deliver a faulty component of the service, this could cause greater harm to the delivery of the service. Organizations should understand that the entire service lifecycle value chain needs to be assessed and measured for service improvements so that IT service constraints are not created and the expected value is delivered. So, improving one aspect of the service such as a particular process without regard for the other processes in the value chain may improve the particular process but not the overall service management practice and not the IT services. The adverse impact of such actions can be significant to the business.

The service lifecycle, as shown in Figure 5.1, illustrates the point that continual service improvement provides feedback to other stages of the lifecycle, which can be helpful in identifying and undertaking improvement. For example, if an operational service is found to need improvement, the changes for improvement may need to go through transition to implement the (simple) improvement or back to service design to design the improvement appropriately. Related strategy process improvements may also need to be considered. This measurement and improvement initiative can also help with future improvements for other services. The organization should consider improvements not just in terms of a specific service or process, but because of the possible positive impact on other services.

7.1 MEASURING AND DEMONSTRATING BUSINESS VALUE

Figure 7.1 shows why we measure. The simple reasons why we measure are to find out whether the service is behaving as required (which validates our strategy), to direct actions with targets and metrics, to justify changes with factual evidence, and to intervene with changes to meet the target goals.

Business outcomes are defined as part of strategy and service metrics related to these outcomes are defined during service design. Organizations sometimes use expert opinion or the opinions of employees or partners to help inform decisions for service improvements. These opinions are based on experiences. Sometimes organizations use metrics alone without expert opinion. This can be misleading, especially when the measures relate to coordination with business outcomes and overall business strategy. Using expert opinion and metrics together is best for achieving the organizational strategy. For example, based on current metrics and trend analysis, a capacity manager discovers that the organization will run out of disk space in three months' time. After understanding the expert opinion from a business analyst of the service that uses the disk space, the capacity manager discovers that the disk drives are sized appropriately for the business strategy and no additional capacity is needed because the current capacity is perfect for the expected patterns of business activity. The capacity manager was not aware of the patterns of business activity and without that expert opinion they would have made the wrong assumptions and taken the wrong action using only the metrics.

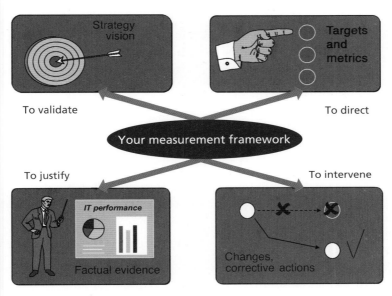

Figure 7.1 Why do we measure?

7.2 DETERMINING AND USING METRICS

There are many types of metrics that can be used. Service providers should take advantage of balanced scorecards and other tools to help them understand the relevance of one key performance indicator (KPI) or metric to another. The service provider should also understand the relevance of key metrics to critical success factors (CSFs). How CSFs relate to objectives, objectives to goals, goals to mission, and mission to overall organizational vision needs to be understood. A challenge here is making sure that the business and IT do not have different objectives, different priorities for objectives, or competing objectives. A disparity such as this between IT and the business will result in IT services failing to meet customer outcomes and is not good-practice service management. If the proper lifecycle processes are followed, then common objectives will be taken into account in service strategy and design, with the result that the metrics will relate back to these, and the various processes will contribute to ensuring that this view is maintained. Otherwise, if a service provider does not relate IT metrics to business outcomes properly, the result will be ineffective metrics and it will appear that the business and IT are not aligned.

Technology, process and service metrics support continual service improvement. Technology metrics are associated with performance, availability etc. Process metrics are associated with the health of a process and take the form of CSFs, KPIs and activities related to the process. Process metrics help identify improvement opportunities for a process and are usually obtained through process-level assessments such as those done during an ISO/IEC 20000 assessment. Service metrics are a measurement of the end-to-end service performance. The technology and process metrics help in determining the end-to-end service performance. Organizations that do not create service metrics will focus only on technology or process changes that may not affect the overall service performance.

Tension metrics can help teams perform better. Tension metrics are resources, functionality and time balanced, with trade-offs among the three areas. For example, these metrics would help with the delivery of a service development project to meet business requirements within time constraints, budget and scope.

Metrics can also be classified into financial, learning and growth, and organizational effectiveness. These metrics can help with determining service quality and should also be used in measuring the effectiveness of IT staff. They should be results-focused and should be included at strategic, tactical and operational levels in the organization. These metrics can help relate IT efforts to business outcomes. The entire service value chain should contribute to these metrics across the service lifecycle.

When interpreting metrics it is important not just to take the metrics at face value but to apply expert opinions to them and to other factors such as changes to environment or service. Service providers should question why the metrics show what they show. People within the organization with knowledge of trends, rumours and changes can help with their expert opinions. Although opinions are sought, there should also be due diligence to quantify the knowledge.

7.3 DESIGN AND DEVELOPMENT OF MEASUREMENT FRAMEWORKS

A service measurement framework is a set of measurements used to measure service impact, efficiency, performance and overall return on investment (ROI) to create an IT scorecard. The framework should define what success looks like for the organization. The purpose of a service measurement framework is to add value to the process of decision-making. It is very important to pick appropriate metrics, but this task is quite hard. Initially, organizations may pick the wrong metrics for measuring service outcomes. The data needed for outcomes such as 'improve service performance' is very difficult to decide. Some data can be unobtainable if no method to measure it is available.

Developing a service measurement framework requires:

- An understanding of business services/processes, including:
  - The current and desired business state
  - Service level agreements
  - What success looks like
- Having IT goals and objectives that support the business, which depend on:
  - Defined roles and responsibilities (Responsible, Accountable, Consulted and Informed – RACI)
  - Established relationships between IT services and business services
  - Integrated business planning with IT
- Understanding past, current and future outcomes which inform:
  - Why, what, how and when to measure.

Understanding organizational maturity is also important when choosing (and using) metrics to help determine the future state of services delivered. Organizations that are immature are not capable of supporting sophisticated metrics and should keep their metrics very simple. When designing measurement methods, they should be fit for purpose (utility) and fit for use (warranty).

KPIs supported by metrics need to support high-level goals. KPIs should be based on compliance, quality, performance and value. A high-level goal could be to 'Improve service value by the end of the year'. To accomplish this goal, an organization may want to reduce the cost of a service because the ROI is not what was expected. In this case, metrics related to cost, price and customer value perspective may be helpful. The organization may choose a Type III provider if it is currently using a Type I or II provider for the service, to reduce the cost. Metrics should include progress towards goals, compliance with governance, and effectiveness and efficiency of process.

Organizations may find that they do not have specific metrics related to the current state of the service. These organizations sometimes use the term 'good enough' until they are able to specifically measure their capabilities and delivered outcomes. This in itself can lead to improvements in the metrics framework, monitoring and the services themselves.

7.4 MONITORING AND CONTROL SYSTEMS

Services and service assets need to be monitored so that their capabilities are understood. Monitoring also helps in the detection of changes from a desired state because of configuration drift. Drift can happen if unauthorized changes have been made to the IT environment or due to unforeseen use outside the normal processing ranges.

Value-added reporting of key metrics obtained from monitoring can help organizations understand normal behaviour and help maintain operational value when changes are made. Organizations may want to put in certain controls when an abnormality to the desired current state happens. These controls are monitor control loops. Based on an activity, IT monitors the activity and then compares it to the normal activity to determine whether corrective action needs to take place to bring the IT system or process back to the desired state. Without this monitoring and control activity being in place in operations, the organization is at risk of not meeting its business requirements.

There are two types of monitor control loops: open- and closed-loop systems. Most organizations prefer open-loop systems to closed-loop systems. Open-loop systems perform specific activities without looking for exceptions such as environment changes. Closed-loop systems monitor an environment and respond to changes in the environment. As closed-loop systems detect changes in environment, organizations create open-loop systems to always respond to that activity in a particular manner. This increases the number of open-loop responses based on predictive activities. For example: an exception occurs during a defined process and the IT staff performing the process consult with the process owner on a course of action that is not documented; this exception continues to occur each week and the process owner decides on a course of action; the process owner eventually makes the exception processing a part of the normal process, so that the IT staff know the course of action; the IT staff then no longer treat the exception as an exception but as part of the normal process. This helps with the overall performance of the IT staff.

7.5 USE OF EVENT MANAGEMENT TOOLS

Event management tools help automate the detection of activities and the response to those activities. The more mature the event management systems become, based on closed-loop interactions, the more open-loop rules are put in place to manage events. For example, as the IT staff responsible for event management understand the course of action for various events, instead of basic routeing to incident management, the staff may route events to problem management or change management. This change in routeing is due to IT staff understanding that when a particular event occurs, it always requires a change in the system, so the event is sent immediately to change management, bypassing incident and problem management. This will improve the performance of event handling and the overall maturity of event processing.

Events can be categorized into informational, warning or exception events using the event management tools, based on knowledge from IT staff or previous closed-loop interactions. This will help with providing appropriate process or people responses from incident, problem or change management.

7.6 SUMMARY

MALC06 focuses on measurement. Measurement is important for understanding the current state of IT services, for ensuring that objectives are being met and for creating appropriate targets for the desired state of a service based on improvement efforts. Many types of metric are used to help validate, justify, direct and intervene in the management of services. Metrics have to be monitored at established set intervals to provide value for service, process and technology decisions. Metrics help service providers and their customers to understand the current service state, and organizations to develop appropriate future improvements that will add business value.

Implementing and improving service management capability

8 Implementing and improving service management capability

This is learning unit ITIL EX: MALC07 of the syllabus. The recommended minimum teaching time is 4.5 hours. This unit represents how to assess service management maturity and performance in order to inform improvement and organizational change. The unit focuses on the capabilities of implementing the practice of IT service management and improving the practice of service management. Service management as a practice uses ITIL alongside other practices and techniques, such as SWOT (strengths, weaknesses, opportunities and threats) analysis and Six Sigma to achieve service outcomes. Organizations should use the appropriate tools in relationship to their capabilities to address each improvement challenge. Organizations also need to focus on constraints which hinder service improvement across the service value chain. Constraints can be caused by a number of factors, including people, process, technology, governance and politics.

Strategy drives the practice of service management and how services should be managed. Once you have a clear view of what the business is trying to accomplish, you should perform a current capability assessment of your service to provide a baseline and to understand the current service state. This assessment, in conjunction with an understanding of service needs, can help with the identification of gaps and shortfalls in specific areas of the practice and in meeting business outcomes.

The next stage is planning for service improvement, with a focus on quick value wins. It includes the assessment of metrics related to the continual improvement process and gathering and analysing data used to support project and service decisions.

Improvement projects can be discrete projects with the aim of achieving a specific improvement. Alternatively, improvement projects can include a collection of improvements, in which case they would normally be time-boxed, with specific controlled periods of time for determining value or the corrective actions that are needed. Figure 8.1 (from *ITIL Continual Service Improvement*) illustrates the continual service improvement (CSI) approach. This will help you to keep the business strategy in mind when planning your improvement initiatives.

8.1 IMPLEMENTING SERVICE MANAGEMENT

A key consideration in the implementation or improvement of service management is the value of the improvement to the business. Business cases help quantify the value of the improvement. When the return on investment (ROI) is obvious to the stakeholders, the requirement for a documented business case is usually waived in order to expedite the needed changes. An improvement in the current implementation of a service management practice is related to the improvement of one or more services. If no services need improvement based on

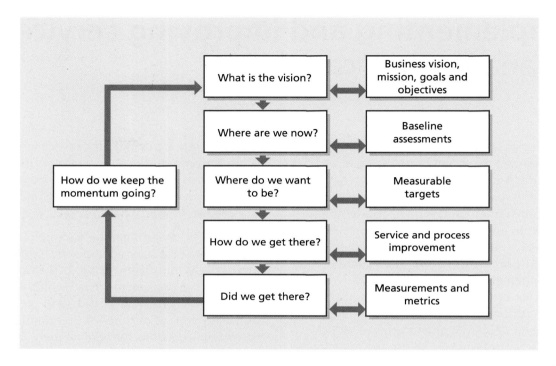

Figure 8.1 Continual service improvement approach

business strategy, then the practice does not need improvement. For example, a chef delivers a service to a customer, simply the preparation of a certain meal; the meal is considered good and of good value; currently there is no competition in the chef's area of business; therefore the chef does not need to change the service or the practice of delivering the service.

There can always be justification for improvement of a service to improve the ROI, total cost of ownership (TCO), value on investment (VOI), return on asset (ROA) or any perceived value. In this case the service management practice will also need to improve to match the needs of the business in the delivery of services.

When implementing service management within an organization, the organization should understand how the changes will affect current strategy, operations and the organization's competitive advantage. A formal strategy for the implementation of service management can be produced using project management best practices. The implementation should include the following areas:

■ **Current state assessment** Baseline the current organizational capabilities
■ **Target state definition** The desired state: what success looks like
■ **Gap analysis** The difference between the current state and the desired state

- **Project identification** The objectives and the activities that need to be done
- **Project estimation** Project scope, time, cost, risks and interdependencies
- **Project consolidation** The organizational changes needed, including governance, people and process changes
- **Roadmap** A time-bound plan with a sequence of activities.

8.2   ASSESSING SERVICE MANAGEMENT

It is always important to understand the current situation related to your practice and processes. There are a number of techniques and best practices, other than ITIL, that can be helpful for service management. You should always use the right tool for the job. Here is a partial list of other techniques and practices that can help:

- **Strategic assessment** Looks at the current state of the organization and the impact of any changes. It gives the organization the ability to review cumulative service impacts and to look for improvement or outcomes on a larger scale related to strategy rather than just at a particular project level
- **SWOT analysis** Identifies internal strengths and weaknesses, and external opportunities and threats. It gives the organization the ability to set achievable goals and objectives to build upon strengths, reduce or eliminate weaknesses, mitigate threats and take opportunities
- **Gap analysis and maturity assessment** Compares current and future states of the business. It gives the organization the ability to assess itself against best practice so that it can decide which areas to improve

- **ISO/IEC 20000** Audits the organization for IT service management compliance, giving it the ability to assess itself against an industry standard for IT service management. Passing the assessment can also give the organization a competitive advantage in the market against organizations that are not ISO/IEC 20000 certified
- **Six Sigma** This process improvement approach gives organizations a best-practice approach for the quality improvement of processes
- **COBIT (Control OBjectives for Information and related Technology)** Taking this governance and control approach is considered best practice for managing risk and delivering value from IT
- **CMMI (Capability Maturity Model Integration)** This process improvement approach is a best-practice tool for organizations to measure and improve service performance, standards and processes
- **Benchmarking** Gives organizations the ability to self-assess their performance, compare themselves with other organizations and better understand their processes for decision-making. It is an assessment tool used for driving strategic change.

8.3   IMPROVING SERVICE MANAGEMENT

When improving service management, organizations should consider potential improvements and decide whether they are required in the short, medium or long term. Improvements can be triggered by events across the lifecycle and by external environmental changes. The CSI register is recommended for tracking suggested improvements. Short-term improvements that are communicated effectively help organizations to obtain buy-in for IT service management initiatives from stakeholders. When people see or hear about successful changes that have an impact on business performance, they are more willing to embrace the changes and to be a part of the changes. Short-term project wins are very important for IT service management programme success.

The continual service improvement approach is the basis for planning short-, medium- and long-term improvements. Each improvement must be justified and should therefore align with the business vision, mission, goals and objectives. If the improvement cannot meet this requirement, it is unlikely to have business value and should not be done. Every improvement that does not contribute business value affects the organization's ability to make one that can. Improvements that do not deliver business value use organizational resources and capabilities that could have been allocated to other projects that could add business value.

Every activity in the continual service improvement approach adds value. The activities help keep the improvement project's cost, time and scope on track. The activities also help create an organizational environment conducive to the practice of service management, where services are delivered successfully based on following the CSI model.

8.4 KEY CONSIDERATIONS FOR IMPLEMENTATION AND IMPROVEMENT

A focus on business outcome has to be maintained. A business case can help the business articulate to IT the expected value, so that no misunderstandings happen. The IT project managers, service owners, process owners and other stakeholders can readily review the document to understand what business outcomes are needed.

The concept of service economics is important. Basically it is the economic value of a service to the organization. For the service to have economic value it must return more value than it costs or indirectly deliver an outcome that is worth the cost. For example, an enhancement to a service provided to external customers may not generate additional value or monies but without the enhancement these customers will seek a different service provider; in this case the service still generates a positive ROI but now, because of the service enhancement, the ROI is lower. The dynamics of service economics consist of three key process areas (service portfolio management, financial management for IT services, and demand management), ROI analysis and a business impact analysis. Services within the portfolio have to be delivered at the right cost; the service provider needs to understand the demand for the services; and these two aspects have to deliver positive ROI. Organizations also have to understand their relative service priorities for resource management and allocations for ROI and VOI. 'Resource' in this context includes funding, people and infrastructure. This type of financial analysis related to service economics is important for ensuring sound business cases.

All stakeholders should be informed of changes as a result of proposed implementations. Communication, roles and responsibilities are important considerations, as changes have to be managed and monitored across the organization and service lifecycle for effectiveness and efficiency. Any external customers or partners, as well as the internal stakeholders within IT and the business, should know about the service changes.

When implementing service management technologies, the organization should make sure that licences are managed appropriately. Licences are given for technology in either a dedicated or a shared manner – dedicated to an individual for their sole use or shared among multiple people who use the technology at the same or different times. Sometimes, if the technology is web-enabled, there may be a need for a web-only licence to support use of the technology. With the advancements in cloud technology, organizations are also using pay-as-you-go or service-on-demand licences to support their service needs. There are also different deployment options for technology implementation, such as 'big bang' or 'phased' implementations of technology. Big bang tends to be used for new implementations and not technology updates.

The practice of service management is based on the business and IT working as one team. Each member of the team has a specialized role to support the delivery of the service. IT should simply be considered a capability of the business that delivers and supports IT services for the core business services. Managing IT services is what IT does on behalf of the business to support business outcomes.

8.5 SUMMARY

MALC07's focus is on implementing and improving service management capability and the practice of service management. Implementing service management capability involves applying the lifecycle to the processes and other components of a service management practice. The improvement of service management as a capability is dependent on understanding the value of the ITIL service lifecycle. Understanding the value helps you to understand what is needed to close gaps in capabilities to solve business issues.

There are assessments and other feedback mechanisms that can help you understand the current state of your services. You can then decide the future state by applying best practice to overcome inadequate capabilities in service delivery or support. Following the CSI approach and the seven-step improvement process can help you to apply best practice to your service improvement efforts. Planning the improvement, checking the status and implementing service improvements will improve not only the services but also the practice of service management.

Applying knowledge to the exam

9 Applying knowledge to the exam

The exam is designed to test your knowledge of ITIL theory and your ability to analyse and evaluate the theory in the context of a case study and specific scenarios. A single case study is used for the exam, and at least eight of the ten questions will refer to the case study. In addition to the case study, each question has a separate short scenario, which needs to be considered for that question only. Each of the exam questions will cover theory from one or more learning units from the syllabus.

MALC is at a higher level than the Intermediate qualifications, which test knowledge at Bloom's level 4. At least five of the ten MALC questions will be at Bloom's level 5. This level requires evaluation and judgement. You will need to use your judgement in order to identify the best way to tackle each question and to determine which information in the case study and which elements of ITIL theory need to be used to answer each question. You should remember that ITIL is non-prescriptive and therefore there is unlikely to be a completely right or wrong answer option based on theory alone. It will depend upon the situation; in other words, the answers to the questions are likely to depend on the information in the case study and the scenario, and not just on the theory.

A common mistake is to consider that a question can be answered using only theory and to ignore the case study. If you answer the question on the basis of theory alone, without taking account of the case study and scenario, then your answer is likely to be incorrect. What might seem a correct answer on the basis of the theory may not be the most appropriate answer when taking into account the situation described in the case study.

Appendix A contains a sample case study, Appendix B contains some practice questions based upon the case study, and Appendix C contains the answers to the practice questions. For each question there is a 'question rationale' explaining the reasoning behind the question and the answer. The questions give examples of some but not all of the styles of questions you might find in a real MALC exam. The rationales show some examples of methods for evaluating the answer options against the theory and the case study, but these are not prescriptive and may not apply to the questions in the real exam. You will need to use your judgement to identify the most appropriate method for each question.

In the real exam, there may be one or two questions that do not use the case study. It will clearly state at the beginning of each question either 'Please refer to the case study' or 'This question does not use the case study'.

The MALC syllabus, which can be found at www.itil-officialsite.com, includes detailed information on the examination format and level of proficiency, as well as a list of terminology, which should be used during course preparation.

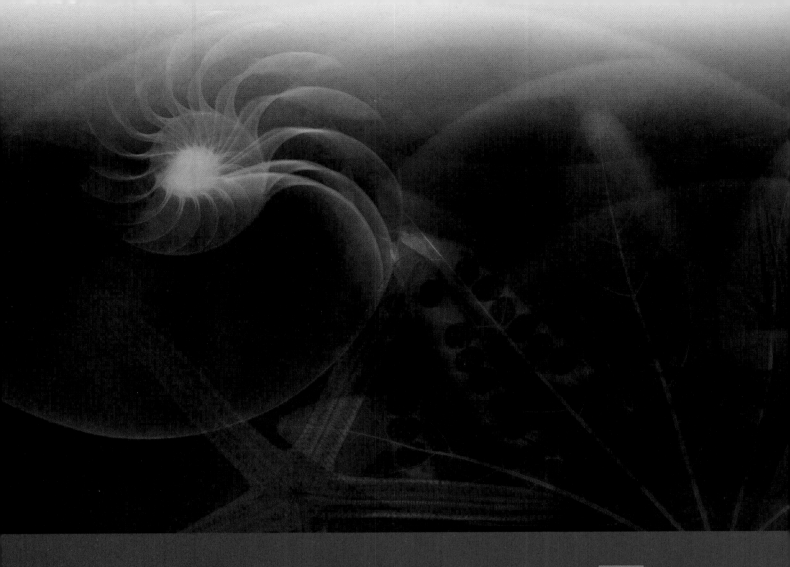

Appendix A:
Sample case study

A

Appendix A: Sample case study

BACKGROUND

A global energy company is involved in the exploration, extraction, storage and distribution of natural gas. It owns natural gas fields in the country where its operational headquarters are based (HQ country) and overseas.

The company owns and manages 65% of the HQ country's natural gas pipelines. These pipelines are used for the transportation and distribution of the gas that the company produces. The company sells its gas both to local distribution companies, for distribution and sale to end consumers, and directly to electricity generation companies. Other suppliers of natural gas have contracts with the global energy company to use its pipelines to distribute their gas.

Overseas, the global energy company does not own pipelines but sells its natural gas to distributors.

BUSINESS PROCESSES

The company's main business processes support:

- Exploration and research, to locate and exploit new gas fields
- Gas extraction, using land-based and offshore drilling platforms
- Pipeline logistics – storage and routeing of natural gas
- Maintenance and engineering of drilling platforms and pipelines
- Regulatory and environmental reporting.

The company is highly regulated. It must meet standards of safety in its operations and maintenance, and must regularly provide information to satisfy regulatory and environmental requirements.

Some aspects of the operation are highly critical to the business. If there is pipeline damage, the appropriate repair must be made quickly to meet safety regulations, to avoid environmental disaster and to prevent significant financial loss. Pipeline maintenance is extremely important and includes both proactive maintenance, such as regular monitoring to prevent leakages, and reactive activities such as emergency repair. Both types of maintenance are supported by IT technology.

COMPANY STRUCTURE

The high-level company organizational structure is set out in Figure A.1.

There are five divisions reporting to the chief executive officer (CEO). A director heads each division. The divisions are:

- Operations division, which has two sub-divisions:
  - Gas sub-division, responsible for gas extraction and processing in the HQ country and overseas
  - Pipeline operations sub-division, responsible for pipeline operations, storage and routeing of natural gas in the HQ country

- Exploration division, responsible for research and exploration in the HQ country and overseas. The small team spends much of its time travelling
- Commercial division, including finance, contracts and marketing departments
- Engineering division, responsible for the maintenance of drilling platforms and pipelines, and for meeting safety regulations. Staff are located in switching centres on the pipelines and on drilling platforms in the HQ country and overseas
- Corporate services division, which includes HR, legal and administration, and IT departments.

The company employs 25,000 people, with 850 of these in the IT department.

CORPORATE VISION AND BUSINESS STRATEGY

The company has grown steadily through successful exploration and the application of its engineering and operational expertise. The corporate vision builds on core strengths and focuses on additional growth through acquisition and diversification.

The company aims to grow by acquiring extraction operations in new overseas markets, where it can exploit its expertise in engineering and operations.

The company has already started to diversify by acquiring some crude-oil pipelines in the HQ country. This acquisition is highly important to the company's growth, and is a major investment for the company.

CHALLENGES, ISSUES AND RISKS

Growth and diversification will present challenges, including:

- Language, time zone and cultural challenges depending on the overseas markets chosen. The plan is to appoint local management and use local contracted staff overseas where appropriate.
- Crude-oil pipelines, including those recently acquired, require additional technology and some additional engineering skills to those used for natural gas pipelines. However, many of the

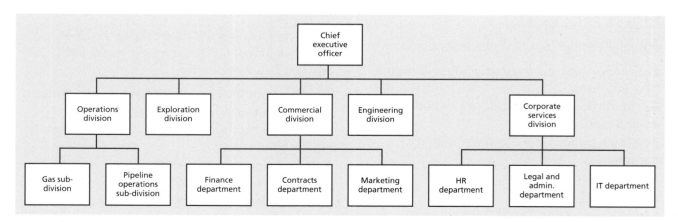

Figure A.1 Organizational structure of global energy company

skills and activities for the two types of pipeline are similar, and the acquisition is expected to provide economies of scale.

■ IT is used to monitor the physical pipelines. Additional IT will be required to support the crude-oil pipelines in order to maximize the benefit from the acquisition. This will require a major programme of work for the IT department over the next year. The implementation of the required IT changes will need to be carefully managed because of the critical nature of the business it supports. Early implementation will be desirable for the business in order to maximize the growth and revenue opportunities.

IT STRUCTURE

The chief information officer (CIO) heads the IT department. The high-level IT organizational structure is set out in Figure A.2.

The IT department is made up of six units, each headed by a manager:

■ IT planning and governance unit, which includes IT strategy and project management.

■ Applications unit, which develops and maintains in-house applications and is responsible for contracts with suppliers of proprietary application packages. This unit also carries out applications management, and second-line and third-line application support.

■ Support unit, which is responsible for two service desks providing first-line support for IT incidents.

■ IT operations unit, which runs the datacentres.

■ Technology unit, which is structured in separate teams for each technical specialism, such as database, network, server, PC etc. The unit includes the pipeline support team, which specializes in the technology for monitoring the pipelines. Each team undertakes technology strategy and architecture, systems programming, procurement of equipment, technical management, and second- and third-line technical support.

■ Security and risk unit, responsible for information security.

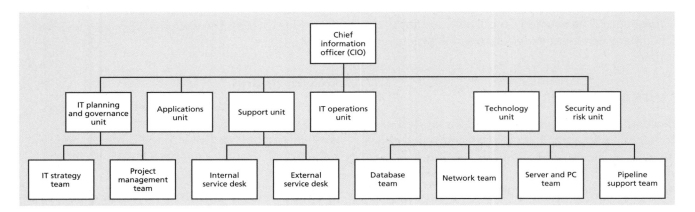

Figure A.2 Organizational structure of IT department

IT SERVICES

A number of IT services are provided to the business. Business processes are directly supported by the following IT services:

- **Process control service to control the processing plants** This is highly specialized and has been outsourced by the engineering division to the third party that supplied the software. The IT department is not involved. The service is business-critical and safety-critical and is very stable and reliable.
- **Pipeline monitoring and logistics service** This is based on technology and software developed in-house and is considered to be a key asset that differentiates the global energy company from its competitors. Most aspects of this service are considered business-critical and safety-critical.
- **Work-planning service, supporting engineering and maintenance activities** Some applications were developed in-house and some by third-party suppliers. Part of this service is business-critical and safety-critical.
- **Regulatory reports service** This includes both applications developed in-house and applications supplied by regulatory bodies, which are updated frequently. The service is important, so that the company can meet its regulatory obligations on time.

IT INFRASTRUCTURE

The company has a primary datacentre located in the HQ building and a back-up datacentre located 100 miles away, providing disaster contingency services. Each datacentre houses a variety of servers and telecommunications equipment.

Each switching centre has a distributed IT environment that is networked to the primary and back-up datacentres. IT technology for monitoring purposes is also located along the pipelines linked to the datacentres through the switching centres.

Across the organization, there are many different types and configurations of PCs in use and some of them are quite old.

IT SERVICE MANAGEMENT SITUATION

The IT department does not formally use ITIL, and the CIO is considering adopting ITIL. There are few documented processes, and different teams take slightly different approaches to their work. Few process areas are formally measured or reported on in terms of their performance.

Service strategy

Unit managers understand their costs, but cost is not measured by service. Business cases are required for major developments, and they focus mainly on the development costs. IT projects often overrun their budgets, because costs relating to service transition and early operation are not planned for.

Relationships with the business work very well but are informal.

Service design

There is no service catalogue, no formal process for service level management and no service level agreements (SLAs) with the business, nor operational level agreements (OLAs) with internal support and service units.

Information security, availability management and capacity management processes are proactive, and are technology-based rather than business-focused.

There are continuity plans in place for some but not all of the critical IT services. The plans are tested on an ad hoc basis.

Supplier management focuses mainly on procurement. Once a contract is in place there is little ongoing supplier management activity.

Service transition

Change management focuses mainly on change approval. Change advisory board (CAB) meetings occur but do not always represent all stakeholders.

There is no configuration management process or system, and this is recognized as a weakness. The operations unit keeps a list of all physical equipment. No one is responsible for software control.

There is no documented release and deployment management process. New applications are usually implemented by the team that developed them. The business often wants new services and changes implemented quickly, which has sometimes resulted in steps being bypassed or cut short, and this has sometimes led to problems when the service is operational.

A recent audit by a software vendor resulted in the company having to pay a large compliance fine because of unauthorized software installations. This created bad publicity, and the CEO has asked that improvements be implemented immediately to prevent a similar occurrence in the future.

Service operation

There are two IT service desks, one supporting customers within the company and one supporting the operations division's external customers in the other organizations that use the company's pipelines. The external service desk was outsourced to a third party six months ago with the aim of obtaining high-quality services for these important external customers. The IT support manager personally manages the relationship with this third party, supported by a signed contract and SLA, including system availability and recovery targets.

There is a documented incident management process, supported by an automated system used by the internal service desk. Measures and reports for the internal service desk activities are well developed, though technically focused. The third-party external service desk has its own automated incident management system, process and separate reporting. It logs and tracks incidents, and reports unsolved incidents and potential problems to the technology unit for resolution.

Staff on the internal service desk have good knowledge of the IT services and, even though they do not use a formal known error database, they keep detailed records of previous incidents, resolutions and workarounds. They resolve a high percentage of incidents at the service desk. This is not the case with the external service desk, which passes the majority of its incidents to the technology unit.

Request fulfilment is undertaken using the internal service desk, enabled with self-help, and users like this service. Requests are not logged and there are no metrics.

The business is becoming dissatisfied with the handling of recurring incidents by the internal service desk. There appears to be a difference between the business and IT perception of priorities.

Problem management is carried out by the teams within the technology unit and is mainly reactive. Members of the technology unit are skilled and knowledgeable, and are usually able to resolve incidents and problems effectively. There are good working relationships between the support unit and the technology unit. The applications unit is very skilled in supporting recently developed applications, but it lacks the skills and knowledge required to support the older work-planning applications. Fortunately the work-planning applications rarely have problems.

Very little automated event management is undertaken. The IT operations unit has high employee turnover caused by morale issues, long working hours and unbalanced schedules.

The access management process is carried out by the security and risk unit using its own automated processes and is proactive.

No formal service reviews with customers take place, and service reporting is informal and ad hoc.

The external service desk recently upgraded its incident management software. Immediately after this upgrade, call response times increased and the call abandon rate increased. Service desk staff tried to work around this by reducing the length of time they gave to each call, resulting in reduced caller satisfaction. The problem was not corrected for several weeks. The degradation in service desk performance had a severe effect on the productivity of the pipeline logistics business unit and caused issues with other organizations using the company's pipelines. However, investigation has shown that the external service desk met the provisions of its contract with the energy company.

The internal service desk team are aware of the issues with the outsourced service desk and they feel that they can do a better job. They believe they have better processes in place, which would enable better service desk performance.

Continual service improvement

Although there is no formal continual service improvement (CSI) process, improvements are identified and introduced from time to time.

IT PROJECTS

A major business programme is under way, to support the strategic acquisition of crude-oil pipelines and their development in the HQ country. The programme sponsor is the engineering director. The programme is being led and run by members of the engineering division and also involves members of the pipeline operations sub-division, which will operate the crude-oil pipelines. The sponsor wants the work to be done quickly and to a good standard. Funding is not seen to be a constraint.

The programme includes the following three projects being undertaken by the IT department. A project manager has been appointed for each project from within the relevant teams. There are a number of interdependencies between the projects and the implementation plans will need to be linked. The three projects are:

- **Pipeline technology development project** The pipeline support team need to adapt existing technology and develop new software to support the crude-oil pipelines and to integrate this with existing pipeline technology and software. This will result in a change to the pipeline monitoring and logistics service. The team is currently discussing requirements with members of the engineering division.
- **Work-planning project** The work-planning service will require significant amendments to some applications in order to incorporate the requirements for the crude-oil pipelines. The engineering division team is currently

investigating the required amendments, and the IT work has not yet started. The applications unit will lead and undertake most of the work on the project. Some amendments will need to be made to applications supplied and supported by third-party suppliers.

- **IT infrastructure expansion project** Additional IT infrastructure, including networking and monitoring facilities, needs to be installed at new switching centres and along the routes of the crude-oil pipelines. Some infrastructure already exists at the acquired sites and this needs to be assessed to determine whether it can be used in the future. If not, it will need to be decommissioned. Members of several teams in the technology unit will be involved in this project.

Appendix B: Sample test questions

B

Appendix B: Sample test questions

QUESTION 1

Please refer to the case study.

The chief information officer (CIO) has recently hired a programme manager whose role is to programme manage the three IT projects which support the acquisition of crude-oil pipelines. The programme manager will report to the CIO.

The CIO has set the following objectives for the programme manager:

- To ensure that the three projects are delivered successfully to the satisfaction of the business sponsor and user departments

- To ensure that the new and changed IT services transition smoothly into operation without major problems and with minimal disruption to other services.

The programme manager is planning their approach to the projects, and has started to identify some possible activities. Some of these include introducing ITIL processes to support the projects.

Taking into account the nature of the projects, the objectives of the CIO and the current situation described in the case study, which of the following options represents the BEST combination of activities to include in the plan?

Activities		Answer options			
		A	B	C	D
1	Introduce a formal business relationship management process to ensure good relationships and communication with key stakeholders in the business	✓	✓		✓
2	Involve the developers in early life support	✓		✓	
3	Introduce a simple design coordination process, which can be improved over time			✓	✓
4	Focus testing on the pipeline technology as this is a business-critical and safety-critical service		✓		✓
5	Involve the work-planning application suppliers in the change advisory board (CAB) for work-planning changes	✓	✓		
6	Develop a good business case which includes operational costs as well as development costs and shows both return on investment (ROI) and value on investment (VOI)	✓	✓		
7	Set up a programme steering group, comprising senior stakeholders from the engineering division and IT department, to oversee the IT programme	✓			✓
8	Hold regular meetings with the programme sponsor and the business and IT stakeholders	✓		✓	
9	Maintain a tight control on costs to avoid programme overruns		✓		✓
10	Involve operational staff in the design and development stages		✓	✓	✓
11	Create service design packages for each of the services being created or changed	✓		✓	

QUESTION 2

Please refer to the case study.

The operations director has received a formal complaint, which they have passed to the chief information officer (CIO) for urgent action.

Investigation has identified that several important external customers are dissatisfied because major incidents they reported to the outsourced external service desk were not resolved as quickly as they required, causing serious business issues. They believe that the resolution of incidents reported by external customers to the external service desk is given a lower priority than incidents reported by internal customers to the internal service desk.

The external service desk has said that it is working to the terms of its contract and it blames the technology unit for not responding quickly with resolutions.

The technology unit says that the external service desk passes all the incidents it receives to the technology unit, whereas the internal service desk resolves a lot of incidents itself. The technology unit often has to re-route incidents from the external service desk to the support unit for proper first-line support.

The technology unit also says that the information it receives from the external service desk is less useful than the information it receives from the internal service desk. It finds the external service desk difficult to contact and it rarely finds someone to speak to who knows about the relevant incident because there are many service desk operatives.

The technology unit says it is confusing receiving incidents and potential problems from two service desks and that it often wastes resources investigating the same issue twice.

What would be the BEST approach for the CIO to take to resolve the complaint, considering the circumstances?

A	The CIO should ask a member of the IT strategy team to lead a strategic review into the external service desk service, including a SWOT analysis, to determine whether the service should be insourced. The review should consider the business impact of the service. This review should involve members of the operations division and the IT department.
B	The CIO should ask the IT support manager to investigate the feasibility of standardizing the two incident management systems. The IT support manager should undertake a review which considers the following alternative options: (1) implementing the external service desk system for the internal service desk, (2) asking the third-party service desk organization to use the internal incident management system for the energy company's incidents, and (3) producing an interface between the two systems to standardize the information transferred between the service desks and IT units in the energy company. An IT steering committee should be established to oversee this review, including representation from the operations division and its external customers.
C	The CIO should ask the IT support manager to work with the technology unit manager to improve the incident management and problem management processes. They should adopt the seven-step improvement process to identify and make the necessary improvements. The IT support manager should negotiate changes to the external service desk contract to reflect the improved processes.
D	The CIO should ask a member of the strategy team to work with members of the support and technology units to document the services offered to external customers, their IT components and relationships, highlighting risks and constraints. They should work with the operations division to develop a suitable service level agreement (SLA) for these services. The IT support manager should negotiate underpinning operational level agreements (OLAs) and any required changes to the external service desk contract and SLA. The CIO should act as a two-way communication link with the business.

QUESTION 3

Please refer to the case study.

The chief information officer (CIO) has arranged for an independent maturity assessment to be undertaken, comparing IT service management practice in the global energy company with ITIL best practice. The maturity ratings for the processes assessed are shown in Table B.1.

Ratings have been given on a scale of 1 through 5, where a rating of 1 would indicate that the process is very immature and a rating of 5 would indicate that the process is mature and adding business value. The CIO considers a rating of 2.5 or above to be satisfactory.

The processes marked 'N/A' were not included in the scope of assessment and are not currently undertaken to any great extent.

The CIO wishes to improve processes and adopt ITIL best practice where possible. The activity will be resource-constrained, so the CIO has decided to take a phased approach. The choice of processes to introduce during the first phase will need to take account of the situation described in the case study, including the programme of work.

Table B.1 Processes and maturity ratings for Question 3

Process no.	Process	Maturity rating
1	Strategy management for IT services	N/A
2	Service portfolio management	N/A
3	Business relationship management	2.1
4	IT financial management	2.2
5	Demand management	1.9
6	Design coordination	N/A
7	Service catalogue management	N/A
8	Service level management	N/A
9	IT service continuity management	2.3
10	Capacity management	3.1
11	Availability management	3.1
12	Information security management	3.1
13	Supplier management	2.6
14	Service asset and configuration management	N/A
15	Change management	1.8
16	Release and deployment management	1.7
17	Incident management	2.0
18	Problem management	1.9
19	Request fulfilment	2.7
20	Access management	3.2
21	Seven-step improvement process	N/A

Which of the following answer options represents the MOST appropriate combination of ITIL processes to focus on during the first phase?

A	7, 8, 14, 21
B	8, 14, 15, 16
C	5, 16, 17, 18
D	1, 2, 7, 21

Appendix C: Answers to sample test questions

C

Appendix C: Answers to sample test questions

QUESTION 1

Rationale

Each of the activities in the list needs to be evaluated in terms of:

- Whether it will help towards the objectives set by the chief information officer (CIO), as measured by:
  - Success of the programme
  - Satisfaction of key business stakeholders
  - Smooth transition into operation, with minimal problems for these and other services
- Whether it will address points in the case study relevant to the current situation, and whether these are important points in the context of this programme.

Relevant points made in the case study include:

- Business cases tend to focus on development costs – however, funding is not seen as an issue for this programme, and the programme is strategic and already decided.
- IT projects tend to overrun their budgets – however, cost is not likely to be an issue, and quality and timeliness are more important to this programme.
- Relationships with the business are informal but work well.
- Different teams approach processes inconsistently – this could be an issue for this programme, which will involve several teams.

- IT operations unit staff are demotivated and there is high turnover.
- Applications unit staff are involved in implementing what they have developed.
- The applications unit also undertakes applications management and support, yet it lacks the skills to support the work-planning service – this implies it will face problems in developing or updating this service.
- There is little ongoing management of suppliers.
- The business tends to want early delivery of projects, which can lead to bypassing steps or cutting corners.

Based on these points, Table C.1 rates each of the activities as of HIGH, MEDIUM or LOW positive impact, NO impact or NEGATIVE impact. For example, high impact would be if the activity contributed strongly to the objectives and was also relevant in the context of the current situation in terms of addressing specific issues. Medium impact would be if it contributed to the objectives and addressed issues. Low impact would be if it somewhat contributed to objectives or addressed issues. (Note that this is but one approach to categorization in order to distinguish and rank the answer options; the candidate will almost certainly use a different scheme, which is perfectly acceptable, as long as they achieve the correct answer.)

Table C.1 Assessment of answer options for Question 1

1	Introduce a formal business relationship management process to ensure good relationships and communication with key stakeholders in the business.
	This is best practice and could help to contribute towards the objectives relating to stakeholder satisfaction. However, business relationships already work well and therefore the overall impact of this activity is likely to be relatively LOW.
2	Involve the developers in early life support.
	This is best practice and will contribute towards objectives by helping to minimize problems when first operational. It will be appropriate because development teams are involved during transition. Impact is rated as MEDIUM.
3	Introduce a simple design coordination process, which can be improved over time.
	Design coordination is best practice, which will help to ensure consistency of process between different teams involved in design and development, and will contribute towards objectives. Impact is rated as MEDIUM.
4	Focus testing on the pipeline technology as this is a business-critical and safety-critical service.
	Certainly testing needs to include the pipeline technology, and this is likely to be very important, but other aspects of the changes are likely to be equally important, particularly as the changes are interlinked. In particular, the applications unit faces problems in supporting the older work-planning applications, so this may require a specific focus during testing. Testing plans will emerge during design and development. Deciding to focus testing in this way at this early stage of the programme would be likely to have a NEGATIVE impact.
5	Involve the work-planning application suppliers in the change advisory board (CAB) for work-planning changes.
	As the developers of these changes, it may be appropriate to involve the suppliers in this way, and this might indirectly contribute to minimizing operational problems. Impact is rated as LOW.
6	Develop a good business case which includes operational costs as well as development costs and shows both return on investment (ROI) and value on investment (VOI).
	While this is best practice, this programme is strategic and has already been given the go-ahead. While it would contribute to the longer-term aspects of value delivery, and could help in terms of focusing the business's attention on this if they try to bypass or cut short part of the programme, this activity would provide LOW impact.
7	Set up a programme steering group, comprising senior stakeholders from the engineering division and IT department, to oversee the IT programme.
	There may be an overall business programme steering group; it is not clear from the case study. Certainly, having a steering group for the IT part of the programme might help with the objective of customer satisfaction and overall involvement of the business during relevant parts of the programme. Impact is seen as MEDIUM.
8	Hold regular meetings with the programme sponsor and the business and IT stakeholders.
	This is important, and possibly an alternative approach to a steering group. Impact is rated as MEDIUM.
9	Maintain a tight control on costs to avoid programme overruns.
	This is usually a good approach, but funding is not seen as an issue for this programme; the quality of delivery and timeliness are seen as more important. Focusing on costs could be at the expense of delivery quality and timeliness, so this is seen as having a NEGATIVE impact in this instance.

10   Involve operational staff in the design and development stages.

This is best practice in terms of the early involvement of staff in planning for transition and operation. Developers tend to implement, so operational staff will mainly need to be involved to prepare for operation and support. Operational staff are demotivated, and their involvement in an important programme could help with this, particularly to reinforce their role. It could also help to ensure the objective of minimal problems once the changes are operational. Impact is rated as HIGH.

11   Create service design packages for each of the services being created or changed.

This is best practice and an approach that would help with consistency of process between the different teams involved. It would also help towards all the objectives. Impact is seen as HIGH.

In order of correctness, the options listed in Table C.2 represent the best combination of activities to include in the project plan as described in Question 1.

Table C.2 Answer options and rationales for Question 1

MOST CORRECT (5)	C	This option includes activities with impact as follows:
		● 2 High
		● 3 Medium
		● 1 Low
SECOND BEST (3)	A	This option includes activities with impact as follows:
		● 1 High
		● 3 Medium (could be considered as 2 Medium since activities 7 and 8 would have overlapping impacts)
		● 2 Low
THIRD BEST (1)	D	This option includes activities with impact as follows:
		● 1 High
		● 2 Medium
		● 1 Low
		● 2 Negative
DISTRACTER (0)	B	This option includes activities with impact as follows:
		● 1 High
		● 3 Low
		● 2 Negative

Syllabus unit/module supported/subjects covered

- MALC04 Managing services across the service lifecycle – all subjects, with particular attention to the stages of service design through transition into operation
- MALC02 Communication and stakeholder management.

Testing level/link to case study/level of difficulty

Bloom's taxonomy testing level: 5

Link to case study: medium to strong

Difficulty: hard

QUESTION 2

Rationale

The case study and scenario describe a confused picture in terms of how the core service (related to pipeline monitoring and logistics) is delivered by IT and its various teams, including the outsourced external service desk. There are skills in the internal service desk and the technology unit that are of value to the service, but there are shortcomings in the supplier management of the external service desk, and the case study implies that there may also be shortcomings in the external service desk contract and service level agreement (SLA), and inconsistent communication between all parties.

While the external service desk might appear to be at fault at first glance, the question scenario reveals that it says it is meeting the terms of its contract, and the case study reinforces that the issues might relate to the contract and SLA and/or supplier management, which is not carried out to any extent once contracts are operational. Therefore we cannot be certain the external service desk is to blame for the issues. In any case, the external service desk is 'personally managed' by the IT support manager, who should be taking responsibility for ensuring it provides an appropriate supporting service.

Having two service desks effectively dealing with the same incidents for two sets of customers is likely to cause issues unless there is a good means of sharing and communicating, such as through a shared incident management system or strong communication between the two desks. This does not appear to happen in this case. There also appears to be some ill-feeling on the part of the internal service desk.

An ideal option would be to deal with the immediate issues (addressing the complaint which requires urgent action) and then to take a longer-term, more strategic approach to resolving the underlying problems, linking the services, and designing a better structure and process for incident and problem management. None of the options offers this. We have to make a judgement as to whether it is better to take a strategic approach or a more tactical one in the circumstances.

Relevant points from the case study and scenario include:

- The strategic nature of the services and the importance of the customers involved
- The fact that the complaint requires urgent action
- The lack of service level management, SLAs with the business, or operational level agreements (OLAs) and consistent targets with internal units
- The recent problems with the external service desk and ill-feeling from the internal service desk

- The fact that the external service desk has only been outsourced for six months
- The skill of the internal service desk in being proactive and resolving incidents at the desk, and of the technology unit in resolving problems
- The internal focus of the internal service desk

- The differences between the IT and business view of priorities regarding incidents.

In order of correctness, the options in Table C.3 represent the best approach for the chief information officer (CIO) to take.

Table C.3 Answer options and rationales for Question 2

MOST CORRECT (5)	D	This option gets to the heart of the issues, taking a business-focused perspective. It focuses on understanding the relationship between the core service to the business and underpinning elements/enabling services involving the two service desks and other parts of IT, in order to identify constraints to delivering business value from the service. There are a lot of service components and the relationships are not clear.
		Developing an SLA will help set the business expectations, and provide a basis for improvements that might need to come later. Setting appropriate targets for those involved in delivering the service will help to ensure that their delivery is focused appropriately, and will enable the escalation of major incidents and problems.
		The outsourced service desk's SLA will be negotiated to incorporate these targets. This third party may still not be able to achieve them, but it will be more likely to escalate to the technology unit in a timely fashion, and its contract will be more appropriate based on a contractual SLA which underpins the SLA that the IT department will have with the operations division.
		This option is better than option C because it provides the basis upon which the incident and problem management processes can operate. The processes may be found to require further improvement but the service level targets will in the meantime focus attention to help prevent further issues. This option also involves the business so that the operations division can see and participate in the progress of the complaint.
SECOND BEST (3)	C	It seems clear from the case study and question-based scenario that the incident management process (and its link with problem management) needs to be improved, and that this is a key contributor to the issues. Option C is likely to go some way towards addressing the problems.
		Depending on the details of the incident management process and how it is used by the various parties involved, this option may be achieved relatively quickly or it may take some time to achieve. However, it is likely to be quicker than options A and B.
		This option is not as good as option D because, for the processes to work well, both service desks and support teams will require an understanding of the business impact of incidents, as well as clear targets. Although the contract with the external service desk will be updated to incorporate the improved process, there is nothing in this option that will establish better service levels. There is also nothing in this option to manage stakeholders within the operations division.

THIRD BEST (1)	A	When faced with a set of problems, taking a strategic approach to solve them is usually a good option, and it would be appropriate in this case if there were not an urgent issue that needs to be addressed. Involving relevant members of the business and IT would also be appropriate.

There is likely to be some merit in considering insourcing the external service desk service, since outsourcing strategic or business-critical services to strategic partners brings a number of business risks. This is particularly pertinent considering the global energy company's growth plans. There have also been other problems with the external service desk (possibly not all of their making), and insourcing the service may be found to be the right way forward in the medium term. There are also inevitable risks with having two service desks covering the same services and this approach would identify the options for resolving these risks. We are told in the case study that the service was outsourced six months ago. There might be scope to make improvements in the contract and its SLA before the major step of insourcing the service.

The main issue is that this option will take time, during which nothing is being done to prevent further incidents and complaints.

This option is therefore not as good as option C, because it does not address the immediate issue. However, it is an option that would make sense after the immediate issue is resolved, and it is better than option B because it has merit in the future.

DISTRACTER (0)	B	This option provides a technology-based solution, yet it is not clear that technology is the reason for the problems. The option does not include an investigation to identify whether the incident management systems contribute to the problem; it simply investigates the feasibility of standardizing or interfacing the technology.

There may be many reasons why it is not possible or desirable to standardize the incident management system across the two service desks. If standardizing the system is found not to be possible, then interfacing the systems to standardize the information might address some aspects of the problems, though even this might not be feasible. It would be better to start by considering the information exchanges at the interfaces, rather than the technology.

There is some merit in this option, in that the contract with the external service desk and its SLA will be brought into line with whatever changes are made.

However, having a steering committee include external customers of the operations division, particularly such strategic partners, would be extremely risky and not really appropriate for this type of initiative.

This too is a fairly long-term option, and does nothing to address the urgent complaint in the meantime. It is not as good as option A because it offers only a technical solution, it will not address most of the underlying problems and involving the external customers is not appropriate.

Syllabus unit/module supported/subjects covered

- MALC05 Governance and organization – organizational structure, skills and competence, service provider types and service strategies
- MALC04 Managing services across the service lifecycle – challenges, critical success factors (CSFs) and risks of the service lifecycle stages, potential conflicts and competing issues.

Testing level/link to case study/level of difficulty

Bloom's taxonomy testing level: 5

Link to case study: medium. Some of the pertinent information is contained within the case study and some within the question-specific scenario.

Difficulty: medium

QUESTION 3

Rationale

Evaluation of the answer options needs to take into account the following for the processes included in each option:

- The current status of the process – if the rating is below 2.5 there is definitely room for improvement and if the process is not currently undertaken it is a potential candidate for introduction.
- The importance of the process in terms of its value to the business now and in the short term during the programme of work:
  - The case study highlights a number of recent and current issues and risks that could be addressed through the improvement of processes.

- What impact will the process have on the programme of work, which underpins important business initiatives?
- The combination of processes to be improved and whether there are any constraints in terms of the sequence in which processes are tackled or the timing of improvements.

The organization is immature and there are a lot of processes that need to be improved or introduced. There are limited resources to address this, and therefore the options chosen need to address the most urgent issues and/or opportunities for improved business value.

For each of the processes listed in the answer options, these points have been analysed, taking into account the information in the case study as well as the information in the question-specific scenario. Note that there is no point in analysing the processes that do not appear in at least one of the answer options.

The following points from the case study are relevant:

- The projects and their implementation will require careful management, and this would indicate the importance of a good change management process, and good release and deployment management.
- The business often wants changes implemented quickly, which has resulted in steps being bypassed or cut short, and sometimes leads to operational problems. This would indicate the importance of a good change management process, and good release and deployment management.
- There have been serious issues with software licensing, which have created bad publicity for the organization, and the chief executive

officer (CEO) has asked for improvements to be implemented urgently. The software-control aspects of the service asset and configuration management process would assist in this.

■ A number of the services are business-critical and safety-critical. Introducing service level management could be of value and improving incident management could also be helpful.

■ The business is becoming dissatisfied with recurring incidents that imply a need for an improvement to incident management and/or problem management.

■ There is a difference between the business and IT perception of priorities. This could be addressed by introducing service level management.

■ The lack of a configuration management system is recognized as a weakness.

■ While problem management is largely reactive, problems are usually solved as a result of the skills of the technology unit.

It should be noted that there may be better combinations of processes than those listed in the answer options. However, the choice that has to be made is to identify the most appropriate of the answer options given. (This might reflect a situation where particular resources or capabilities limit the choice of activities available.)

Table C.4 shows an evaluation of each process based on:

■ The current status of the process and the opportunity available for improvement

■ The extent to which the process would help address current risks and issues

■ The extent to which the process will be helpful towards the programme of work.

For each process, the impact of introducing or improving the process has been evaluated as HIGH, MEDIUM, LOW or VERY LOW in terms of the situation described.

Table C.4 Evaluation of processes to include in the first phase (Question 3)

Evaluation of processes within the answer options
1 Strategy management for IT services
This process doesn't exist currently. However, it would not directly address any of the current issues and risks. It might be of some help in determining a strategic approach for the work programme, but it is not really appropriate at this stage.
Overall impact VERY LOW
2 Service portfolio management
This process doesn't exist currently. However, it would not directly address any of the current issues and risks. It is unlikely to provide additional value to the work programme.
Overall impact VERY LOW
5 Demand management
This process is rated as 1.9 and there is scope for improvement. However, it would not directly address current issues and risks or add value to the work programme.
Overall impact VERY LOW

7	Service catalogue management

This process does not exist currently. It would not directly address current issues and risks. It might add some value to the work programme in terms of documenting the resulting services and supporting service level management.

Overall impact LOW (or MEDIUM if implemented with service level management)

8	Service level management

This process does not exist currently. It would have an impact on current risks relating to critical services and differences between business and IT perception of priorities, and it is likely to be helpful in supporting the work programme for similar reasons.

Overall impact HIGH

14	Service asset and configuration management

This process does not exist currently. Its introduction would help address the urgent issues and risks relating to software licensing (although it would not require the whole process to be implemented) and it may be helpful in supporting the work programme and other processes.

Overall impact MEDIUM

15	Change management

This process is rated as 1.8, so there is scope for improvement. It would address current issues relating to bypassing steps and would be important for managing the work programme and its implementation.

Overall impact HIGH

16	Release and deployment management

This process is rated as 1.7, so there is scope for improvement. It would indirectly help with some of the current issues relating to bypassing steps and would be important for the work programme and its implementation.

Overall impact HIGH

17	Incident management

This process is rated as 2.0, so there is some scope for improvement. Improvement would address the current issues with recurring incidents, although it would not directly add value to the work programme.

Overall impact LOW

18	Problem management

This process is rated as 1.9, so there is some scope for improvement. The process is reactive but this is not considered to be a risk since problems are being resolved. There are recurring incidents, which might be addressed by improved problem management. However, it would not directly add value to the work programme.

Overall impact LOW

Table continues

Table C.4 *continued*

21	Seven-step improvement process
	This process does not exist currently. However, its introduction would not address any current issues. Although it is unlikely to be directly helpful for the work programme supporting the business, it could be helpful in supporting these process improvements.
	Overall impact MEDIUM

This relatively simple approach to scoring the processes gives impact levels for the answer options as shown in Table C.5.

Table C.5 Impact levels for answer options (Question 3)

A	1 High and 3 Medium
B	3 High and 1 Medium
C	1 High, 2 Low and 1 Very Low
D	1 Medium, 1 Low and 2 Very Low

It is also important to consider the combination of processes in each answer option, to consider any constraints or benefits relating to improving these processes as a group, and to compare the answer options against each other. For example, some processes require a lot of effort and time to implement, while others may be introduced relatively quickly. It can be easier to improve an existing process than to create one from scratch, although it will depend on the process concerned and the existing situation.

In order of correctness, Table C.6 gives answer options and rationales for Question 3.

Table C.6 Answer options and rationales for Question 3

MOST CORRECT (5)	B	These processes will address some of the current issues and help to ensure that the changes relating to the work programme are controlled and implemented in accordance with good practice, providing business value. This combination of processes also works well because, for example, a good change management process will be essential to control configuration changes, and the change management and release and deployment management processes can be aligned. The work programme is extremely important to the company and will require good control processes.
SECOND BEST (3)	A	Three of these processes will help to address current issues and two will support the programme of work or these process improvements. This option is not as good as option B because there is a risk that the current change management and release and deployment management processes are not good enough to support the important changes coming with the work programme.

| THIRD BEST (1) | C | This option focuses on processes that are currently carried out to some extent but have rated poorly in the assessment. It includes three processes which, if improved, could address some existing issues and one which will have positive value for the programme of work. |
| DISTRACTER (0) | D | This option focuses on processes that currently do not exist. This combination is not as good as option C because these processes are less important in the current situation in terms of addressing issues and/or supporting the work programme. |

Syllabus unit/module supported/subjects covered

- MALC07 Implementing and improving service management capability
- MALC03 Integrating service management processes across the service lifecycle – the value to business of processes.

Testing level/link to case study/level of difficulty

Bloom's taxonomy testing level: 5

Link to case study: medium

Difficulty: easy

Index

Index